CHINA AFTER MAO

Leslie Evans

Monad Press, New York

Copyright © 1978 by the Anchor Foundation, Inc.
All rights reserved
Library of Congress Catalog Card Number 78-59264
ISBN 0-913460-61-3 cloth; ISBN 0-913460-62-1 paper
Printed in the United States of America

Published by Monad Press for the Anchor Foundation
Distributed by Pathfinder Press
410 West Street
New York, N.Y. 10014

First printing, 1978

Contents

Charts and Tables

Introduction

The Chinese revolution of 1949 and the People's Republic that issued from it are anomalous phenomena that have puzzled many observers and given rise to very divergent appraisals. The question of China has become highly charged with political passion. That is not to be wondered at. The French, American, and Russian revolutions for a time made the very names of those countries synonymous with the revolutionary overturn of the old order. So it has been with China.

But France, the United States, and even Russia fall within a relatively homogeneous cultural and historical bloc, which gives itself the name *Western civilization*. Contacts are frequent, there is a significant interchange of populations, and many parallel customs and institutions serve to make these countries and their experiences mutually accessible and familiar.

It is otherwise with China. Its ancient civilization lies outside that perimeter. Cut off by geography and language, China has gone its own way for millennia. It has only in recent historical times become part of the "known world"—that is, known to Europeans. Contrariwise, until the last few centuries Europe was for China only a legend of exotic barbarian lands. The very name of China in its language—*Chung-kuo,* the Middle Kingdom—captures the traditional Chinese view of the world. This was not the middle of betwixt and between, but *the* middle, the center of the earth.

Nor was this an idle boast. From the time of its unification in 221 B.C. under Ch'in Shih Hwang, China was matched in geographic extent and population only by the Roman empire at its height. With the fall of Rome, China stood unrivaled not only in the stability of its government but in the standard of living of its people and the extent of its scientific and literary pursuits.

Until a mere two hundred years ago, more books had been published in Chinese than in all of the world's other languages combined. Yet even today, with the exception of the works of Mao—which are circulated in enormous editions by Peking—and two or three classical novels, Chinese literature remains virtually unknown in the West except to specialists. The average literate European or American can discuss the daily life of Russia or Germany, France or England, at least from accounts by these countries' writers. The same is not true, by and large, of China.

If the West was long ignorant of China, the centralized Chinese state was no more inclined to initiate contacts with the West. The self-contained character of Chinese culture, epitomized by the Great Wall erected by the Ch'in dynasty, is derived from the sheer size and breadth of the country, which for centuries did appear self-sufficient in everything. It was not until the industrial revolution of the nineteenth century that newly born Western capitalism gained a sufficient edge on China for the Western "foreign devils" to impose their will on China by force. That humiliating experience hardened traditional Chinese pride into a fierce nationalism that succeeded in 1949 in expelling foreign influences and their agents.

The traditional attitude of the Chinese state to the West can be best seen in the first contacts at the governmental level. In 1793, King George III, following his defeat at the hands of the American colonists, sent Lord Macartney to Peking in hopes of making inroads into the Chinese market. The peer, assuming a modest stance, arrived in Peking with retainers who carried banners in Chinese which read, "Envoy bearing tribute from the country of England."

China, then at the peak of its power and prosperity under Emperor Ch'ien Lung, replied to the English king as though to a barbarian vassal. In his Imperial Mandates to King George, Ch'ien Lung declared:

> You, O King, live beyond the confines of many seas, nevertheless, impelled by your humble desire to partake of the benefits of our civilization, you have dispatched a mission respectfully bearing your memorial. . . .
> If I have commanded that the tribute offerings sent by you, O King, are to be accepted, this was solely in consideration for the spirit which prompted you to dispatch them from afar. . . . As your Ambassador can see for himself, we possess all things. I set no value on objects strange or ingenious, and have no use for your country's manufactures.[1]

Except for a more zealous interest in turning a profit at trade, the British ruling class had much the same arrogant attitude toward China. The effect of this mutual isolation was to make each seem mysterious to the other and to make it difficult to weigh the testimony of those few who crossed the frontiers between the two societies.

Thus, when Marco Polo returned to Venice from Peking in 1295, no one believed his stories of the great empire of the East. For centuries after his death the plagiarized and interpolated travelogues of the British charlatan Sir John Mandeville were far more widely read than Marco's true account of life in China.

This might be attributed to the benighted state of European knowledge in the Middle Ages. It is striking, then, that six hundred years after Marco's time, British Sinologue Sir Edmund Backhouse was able to spend a lifetime in Peking forging Chinese government "documents" for the enlightenment of his countrymen at home, and no one was the wiser until long after his death. Backhouse's greatest put-on was his supposed discovery in 1910 of "The Diary of His Excellency Ching-shan." Ching-shan had been a high official of the Chinese court and had died only ten years earlier, in 1900. That Backhouse's forgery could have been believed for a single day is a measure of the ignorance in the West of Chinese ruling circles. No comparable fabrication of memoirs of a famous government personality would have been possible in any Western country.

The result of this relatively sparse contact is that the level of popular gullibility in Europe and America about things Chinese is higher than it would be about a country that was better known. During the cold war the American capitalist press portrayed Maoist China in the most dehumanizing terms. One book published in 1963 and still to be found in the New York Public Library actually bears the title *Mao Tse-tung, Emperor of the Blue Ants*.

At the opposite pole, many young radicals of the 1960s, in rebellion against the injustices of American capitalism, imagined that they saw in present-day China a land of pastoral simplicity that had escaped the alienating effects of industrial society. They were impressed by the genuine achievements of the revolution in freeing China from imperialist domination. But they also admired in an almost mystical way—and on the basis of very little actual knowledge—what they saw as a sense of belonging, of unalienated collective harmony and a commitment to a common social cause that is so sorely absent from American life.

Since 1972, when President Nixon and Chairman Mao cemented a new relationship of mutual cooperation and détente, the capitalist press in America has made a partial turnabout in its treatment of China. Now, although an occasional article reiterates the cold war themes, the picture of China is quite different. It is painted as a highly disciplined and motivated society of thrifty and hard-working people with many skills and talents waging a determined and effective struggle against the considerable poverty that has, since the years of imperialist penetration, been China's lot.

Not all of these contradictory representations are or could be true. Much of what is reported about China, especially in the American mass media, uses China as a metaphor for social and political themes stemming from American conditions, instead of taking China on its own terms or examining the place of the actual China in world politics.

There is nothing new in this. The lack of popular knowledge about China makes it easily adaptable to tendentious propaganda. The starting point of such myth-making, whether admiring or hostile, is the assumption that there is anything so simple as "the Chinese."

Old China, like the West, was stratified into antagonistic classes; the new China still contains clashing social forces. The revolution it underwent in 1949 was the eruption onto the stage of history of the great mass of the oppressed, above all the peasantry, who in ordinary times are the mere objects of ruling class policy. In the course of that outpouring of elemental anger against the privileged classes of the old order, the Chinese revolution became fused with something new in Chinese history: an assault on the very foundations that had always before permitted the old ruling class, sooner or later, to reconsolidate its positions, no matter what shock it had received. That foundation lay in the private ownership of the sources of social wealth: the land and the tools. When landlordism, capitalism, and imperialism were all swept away by the Chinese revolution, China entered onto uncharted waters. It broke out of the stage of historical evolution in which it could be a self-contained Middle Kingdom and became willy-nilly a part of the world socialist revolution.

The world-historic significance of the Chinese revolution in the struggle for socialism has had an incalculable effect on the colonial and semicolonial countries. It was the first successful reversal—outside Europe, and in the globe's most populous nation—of the trend of modern capitalism throughout the world toward colonial enslavement and foreign economic domination.

It showed the capacity of the Chinese workers and peasants to stand up, throw out their imperialist oppressors, and shatter the corrupt regime of Chiang Kai-shek and his Nationalist Party, the Kuomintang. The Chinese revolution was not simply another nationalist uprising. Had it been so, it would not have succeeded in fully winning China's independence, as the sorry postwar record of India and the rest of the nominally independent neocolonies so amply demonstrates.

With the adoption of socialist measures after 1953, the Chinese government of Mao Tsetung was able to begin the creation of a nationalized economy. Breaking not only with the political rule of capital but also with its foundation, private ownership of property, China was able to open a perspective of accelerated economic growth and to initiate social welfare measures unmatched even by many industrially advanced capitalist countries.

These achievements offer hope to the poverty-stricken millions of Asia, Africa, and Latin America as a more progressive form of economic and social organization than the anarchy of private enterprise. In this sense China has confronted earlier than most countries the central social problem of this epoch: the problem of gaining conscious control over the further evolution and development of human society.

Whatever difficulties or distortions exist in China's social fabric today, its socialist revolution has taken it across the gulf that separates the countries of the world between those that have torn themselves out of the world capitalist economy and those that have not yet done so.

This is not a question of disembodied economic models, as many Western economists are prone to imagine—a "statist" versus a "privatist" way of organizing production. The alternatives facing the world today are not reducible to whim or arbitrary choice but flow from the inner drives of social and productive life. They correspond to the needs of warring classes in society.

Underneath the diplomatic language and illusions of détente, world imperialism, personified by the government of the United States, remains an enemy of the Chinese revolution. Not the least of the pressures operating on world capitalism here is its galling exclusion from the Chinese market, comprising a quarter of the human race.

There should be no ambiguity as to right and wrong in this conflict. Any blow aimed at Peking by the world capitalist order is aimed just as much at the workers and peasants of China as at

the Chinese Communist Party (CCP) and its government. Socialists everywhere have the elementary responsibility to side with
China in this struggle, to make its cause their own, and to act as
allies of the Chinese people at every encroachment on their rights
or threat to their welfare made by Washington. Moreover, their
government has the right to be recognized and placed on a par
with any other.

However, the achievements of the Chinese revolution and the
need to uphold them are only one side of the historical picture of
the last twenty-nine years. The other is the character of the
Chinese Communist Party regime—its social roots and the forces
that have shaped it. Marxists take into consideration both of
these realities and their interaction. Defense of the Chinese
workers' state, yes. But with revolutionary methods.

Here the most dramatic internal contradiction emerges. On the
basis of a historic emancipating revolution made by great masses
of the oppressed has arisen a government that by any objective
measure must be counted among the more repressive in the world.
And in recent years its repression has been directed first and
foremost not at its acknowledged enemies, the proponents of
capitalist counterrevolution within its borders, but at the very
workers and peasants for whom it claims to speak.

To ignore or deny this easily verifiable fact is to become a
cheerleader for the CCP apparatus. This position, as I hope to
show, is incompatible with the aspirations and needs of China's
working masses and with the real requirements of the struggle
for socialism in China and the world.

In recent times a sizable group of Western China scholars of
more of less radical persuasion has emerged. Many are quite
positive in their overall assessment of the experiences and
performance of the Mao regime. Some have a certain admiration,
even reverence, for Mao. Others are somewhat more critical.

This has made possible the assembling of much valuable
information about the People's Republic of China, and many
worthwhile specialized studies have appeared, a number of which
I have drawn on in this work.

What is generally missing is an underlying conception of the
dynamics of the Chinese revolution, the class forces it has set in
motion, the role and viability of its present ruling group, its place
and performance in the world class struggle.

What, then, is the major theme of this book? Above all it is that
Marx's writings on the Paris Commune, Lenin's *State and
Revolution,* and Trotsky's *Revolution Betrayed* are not outmoded

in their authors' common conviction that socialism and democracy are inseparable, or conversely, that socialism and uncontrolled bureaucracy are incompatible. The experience of the decades since the overturn of capitalism in China graphically demonstrates that the Maoist bureaucracy has been more a brake on China's development than an accelerator. Far from being the embodiment of the revolutionary aspirations of China's masses, Maoism has come to be essentially a defender of a new status quo established on a higher socio-economic level. The basis of that regime is the emergence of a highly privileged and conservative social layer of functionaries and administrators who guard their standard of living against the incursions of workers and peasants.

Such a bureaucratic caste appeared first in history in the Soviet Union, in the Stalinist counterrevolution against Lenin and Trotsky's Bolshevik Party. In many respects the Mao regime is derivative of Soviet Stalinism in its origins, methods, and outlook, despite the national rift that today separates the two states.

It is my contention that the Maoist bureaucracy is not only morally at odds with socialism and communism, but, more important, that it cannot objectively hope to consolidate a long-term place for itself in Chinese society. The reason for this is that it cannot solve, in a way compatible with its own survival, the colossal social and economic problems that face China. This brings the apparatus constantly into conflict with the mass of workers, peasants, and intellectuals, and ultimately will bring about its downfall.

Two years ago, many admirers of Mao and Maoism would have dismissed this viewpoint as patently false, in conflict with what they believed to be an essential harmony between the government and the people of China. Since Mao's death, the new government of Hua Kuo-feng and Teng Hsiao-p'ing has, in an effort to stabilize its own power, revealed many harsh truths about China under Mao. These bitter pills have not been sweetened much by coating them with the euphemism that the ills were all the fault of a "gang of four," while Mao and the rest of the party leadership stood by with folded hands.

The period China is going through today, like the post-Stalin period in Russia, is one from which much can be learned. It will tell us a great deal about this central dynamic of present-day China: the tension between its strides forward on the postcapitalist road and the bureaucracy that still holds the reins.

The analysis in these pages, while aiming to do justice to the impressive advances and the still greater potential of the Chinese revolution, aims to present the facts in the situation, so far as these are available abroad, truthfully and without prejudice, from a Marxist standpoint.

Leslie Evans
September 1978

Part I

The Purge

1. A Monument to Mao

Two years after the death of Mao Tsetung, his body lies enshrined in its gargantuan mausoleum in Peking's Tien An Men Square. As a structure built to house the remains of a single human being, his tomb is rivaled only by the pyramids of Egypt. It dwarfs the monuments erected by previous generations to China's ancient emperors. The symbolism of this display of conspicuous veneration is not lost on the Chinese public. It is the new government's claim to legitimized continuity as the inheritor of his power.

There is more than a little irony in the building of monuments to Mao in Peking. While Mao's embalmed corpse is displayed in splendor, many of his closest associates and his wife and family are in jail. The policies and campaigns linked to his name and identified as Maoism in the last twelve years are largely abandoned. And, except for Hua Kuo-feng, the government leadership is in the hands of men Mao drove out of the Chinese Communist Party in 1966-67 as "capitalist restorationists" and "counterrevolutionaries."

How much has really changed in China since the death of Mao? How much remains the same? Who are China's new leaders, and why did they arrest Mao's widow, Chiang Ch'ing, now denounced as part of the "gang of four" that allegedly tried to usurp power? What can China's ordinary people—workers, peasants, students, and intellectuals—expect from the government that has succeeded the "Great Helmsman"?

Questions like these can be partly and provisionally answered, though there are limits to what is known about China today. Despite the fact that its 900 million people constitute almost a quarter of the human race, the Chinese government conducts its business with a secrecy matched only by the big capitalist corporations. China is the only major country in the world that issues no statistics, even for its own citizens. Since the Cultural

17

Revolution initiated by Mao in the 1960s, the government has published few magazines and still fewer books, although there are some signs that this is changing. Travel within China is sharply restricted—not only for foreigners, but also for Chinese, who can leave their city of residence only with party-approved travel documents and permits. No debate is allowed in China's newspapers.

The cult of secrecy is so extreme that Chiang Ch'ing was accused of revealing state secrets because in her interviews with American scholar Roxane Witke in 1972 she discussed her private life with Mao and offered her recollections of public figures in China over the last several decades. In most other countries in the world this would come under the heading of memoirs and not of treason.

Still, China is far from unknowable. People do go there. There are official newspapers, which, however spare their content, report certain facts. What is said one year can be compared to what was said the year before. In the last few years there has begun to be a rise of "samizdat" literature—unauthorized leaflets, wall posters, and pamphlets circulated by private citizens.

Great events are difficult to hide. The last two years in China were unusual in the pace and scope of changes—in leaders, in policy, and among the Chinese masses. Much was disclosed about the inner workings of the Chinese Communist Party and about the Mao regime after the Cultural Revolution. A good point to start is the beginning of 1976, the last year of Mao's rule.

2. The Death of Chou En-lai and the Tien An Men Demonstrations

The 1976 New Year's editorial run jointly by the Peking *People's Daily, Red Flag,* and the *Liberation Army Daily* summed up the Maoist line of the previous decade. Its themes provide a useful yardstick to measure the extent of the policy changes after Mao's death. The editorial asserted that "the principal contradiction in socialist society is the contradiction between the proletariat and the bourgeoisie." This was the slogan advanced by Mao during the Cultural Revolution of the 1960s to brand his opponents in the party leadership and dissenters among the masses as class enemies.

The "revolution in literature and art" under the direction of Chiang Ch'ing was hailed as having resulted in "an efflorescence of creative work."

On economic construction, the editorial reaffirmed Mao's line that human willpower, under tight party control, was the principal productive force and could substitute for technology, training, or the extension of the revolution to the advanced capitalist countries. "The Great Proletarian Cultural Revolution is a powerful motive force for the development of the social productive forces in our country," it said, quoting Mao. It added that the national economy should be built "independently and with the initiative in our own hands, through self-reliance." In support of this perspective of building "socialism in one country," a 1965 poem of Mao was cited, whose concluding lines declared: "Nothing is hard in this world / if you dare to scale the heights."

The editorial also announced the beginning of the Fifth Five-Year Plan. After Mao's death, however, it was revealed that the plan drafted under his auspices had been scrapped. It would be a full two years later, at the beginning of 1978, before a new government would be able to agree on an economic plan to replace Mao's unfulfilled one. And by then, while only a few of its targets would be announced, it clearly bore little resemblance to the economic policies that had come to be known as Maoism.

On January 8, 1976, Chou En-lai died of cancer in Peking at the age of seventy-eight. He had been premier of China since the founding of the People's Republic in 1949 and was the best-known leader of the CCP next to Mao Tsetung. His death precipitated a new purge in the party leadership, as Mao and his faction lashed out at many of Chou's close co-workers and supporters. The most prominent victim of the purge was Teng Hsiao-p'ing.

At the time of Chou's death, Teng was acting as premier—given Chou's illness and Mao's feebleness, he was in effect the day-to-day head of China's government. Yet only a few years before, Teng had been declared by Mao himself to be a traitor and an enemy of the people.

Teng Hsiao-p'ing is no newcomer to Chinese Communist politics. He joined the CCP at the age of twenty in an overseas branch in France in 1924. He studied in Moscow in 1926, then returned to China to help carry out Stalin's policy of CCP entry into the Kuomintang, the bourgeois-nationalist party of Chiang Kai-shek. Teng served as a political instructor in the private army of the "Christian General," Hunan warlord Feng Yü-hsiang. When Feng and Chiang Kai-shek joined forces in the late spring of 1927 to massacre the Communists, Teng went into opposition and became a guerrilla fighter. For the next twenty years he served as a political commissar in one or another of the CCP's rural peasant armies.

Teng did not become part of the central party leadership until the mid-1950s, when he was appointed general secretary of the CCP and became one of its leading economic planners. He worked closely with Soviet advisers in reorganizing China's economy along the lines of the USSR. He also was the reporter at the Eighth Party Congress in 1956 on Khrushchev's denunciation of Stalin at the Soviet Twentieth Party Congress earlier that year. Teng endorsed Khrushchev's report, called for eliminating the "cult of the individual" from Chinese party life, and proposed a party constitution that deleted any reference to Mao Tsetung and his thought as the party's guide (such a provision had been put in on Mao's insistence at the previous party congress back in 1945).

From the late 1950s, Teng became closely associated with China's head of state, Liu Shao-ch'i. The two of them clashed with Mao in 1959, when Mao's economic adventures in the Great Leap Forward began to head toward collapse. More openly critical members of the party leadership were purged at that time, but Teng and Liu succeeded in remaining at their posts and bending Peking's economic policies away from some of Mao's projects and back toward the methods used in the USSR. (Soon after, Liu and Teng became prominent spokespersons for Peking in the Sino-Soviet dispute, so their adherence to Moscow's economic policies did not imply political affinity with the Soviet government.)

In 1966, in the so-called Cultural Revolution, Mao broke with Liu and Teng. The two men were stripped of their posts and branded "renegades, traitors, and scabs." Liu reportedly died, in disgrace. Teng, however, was brought back into the government in 1973, despite the fact that such a turnaround placed in obvious doubt the official Maoist explanations of what the Cultural Revolution had been all about.

Mao evidently was willing to accept Teng's "rehabilitation" as long as no real power went with it. But with Chou's death, and Mao's advanced age, Teng stood to inherit the position of top authority in the government. Mao moved quickly for a purge. Teng's last public appearance in Mao's lifetime was at Chou En-lai's funeral, where he gave the eulogy.

On February 7, the government made the surprise announcement that Hua Kuo-feng and not Teng Hsiao-p'ing was to be the new premier. Hua was then very little known, even in China. He had only recently been elevated to the post of head of the secret police after a career as a provincial administrator. Teng was soon under public attack in party-sponsored wall posters.

The immediate issues presented in the attack on Teng were educational and economic policy. Teng was accused of holding a bourgeois line on education because he allegedly proposed that more time should be spent studying science and technology and less in studying the writings of Mao. On the economic front, Teng was linked to a slogan first propounded by Chou En-lai at the Fourth National People's Congress in January 1975: the "Four Modernizations." Chou had called for modernizing agriculture, industry, national defense, and science-technology.

After Chou's death, the slogan of modernization was branded by Mao as revisionist, and Teng was singled out as its principal surviving proponent. By March, Teng was under fire in the Maoist press for supposedly trying to revive the Soviet-style industrial planning he had been associated with before the Cultural Revolution. Teng was accused of seeking large-scale imports of Western technology, favoring wage raises and material incentives to revive the sluggish economy, proposing the technical modernization of the army, and disparaging the rigid censorship in art and literature imposed by Chiang Ch'ing. These charges must have fallen pretty flat, since most of the things Teng was said to be for sounded fairly reasonable.

Two other sins he was accused of were opposing Mao's cutbacks in higher education and opposing the deportation of urban youth to the countryside. The "youth to the countryside" campaign was a highly unpopular measure. This effort, which had been spasmodic since the 1950s, had been upgraded to a massive operation at the end of the Cultural Revolution, when literally millions of radicalized Red Guard youth were summarily shipped to remote areas of the hinterland for "thought remolding."

In the decade after 1968, according to the government's figures, fourteen million urban high school and junior high school graduates were sent to work in the villages. This is a large part of the entire youth generation. The way the system works, those whose conduct is approved by the party are permitted to return to their families after two years. Those considered dubious or troublemakers remain in the countryside, often for life. Since this is not officially considered a punishment, no appeal is possible.

There is no channel through which Chinese citizens could voice their views on these issues. However, an ingenious means of evading the government's restrictions on free expression emerged: demonstrative public mourning for Chou En-lai, as a safe way of indicating disapproval of Mao's regime. The opportunity presented itself with the annual Ch'ing Ming festival at the beginning of April, the traditional period for honoring the dead.

Thousands of people gathered in Peking's Tien An Men Square on April 1, carrying wreaths and poems in memory of Chou En-lai. The idea caught on, and soon residents with a grievance against the government, from the supporters of Chou and Teng to individuals with no ties to the bureaucracy, all came together at Tien An Men.

Each day the crowd grew larger—and bolder. On April 4, in a crowd of tens of thousands, banners were raised attacking Chiang Ch'ing as a Chinese Indira Gandhi and comparing her to the Dowager Empress, the reactionary regent who dominated the last years of the Ch'ing court at the turn of the century. Plainclothes cops were beaten when they tried to arrest impromptu orators who addressed the crowd.

On April 5, the government gave the order to remove the

wreaths and posters. An angry crowd gathered that swelled at its height to more than 100,000. The demonstrators held the square throughout the day, battling police and militia, burning official vehicles, and even invading a militia barracks on the square and razing it.

After dark, tens of thousands of troops were assembled around Tien An Men and the last of the demonstrators—said to number about 3,000—were assaulted with clubs and rifle butts and arrested. An unknown number of the protesters were beaten to death on the spot—a fact later confirmed by wall posters in Peking in January 1977 demanding that the martyrs be avenged.

The official Peking press the next day published a "counter-revolutionary" poem found in the notebook of one of those arrested in the final sweep. It has since become famous as an outcry of protest:

> *Devils howl as we pour out our grief,*
> *We weep but the wolves laugh.*
> *We spill our blood in the memory of the hero;*
> *Raising our brows, we unsheathe our swords.*
> *China is no longer the China of yore,*
> *And the people are no longer wrapped*
> * in sheer ignorance;*
> *Gone for good is Chin Shih Huang's feudal society.**
> *We believe in Marxism-Leninism,*
> *To hell with those scholars who emasculate*
> * Marxism-Leninism!*
> *What we want is genuine Marxism-Leninism.*
> *For the sake of genuine Marxism-Leninism,*
> *We fear not shedding our blood and laying*
> * down our lives;*
> *The day modernization in four fields is realized,*
> *We will come back to offer libations and sacrifices.*[2]

---

*Ch'in Shih Hwang (259-210 B.C.) was the first emperor of China and is generally regarded as one of the greatest despots of all time. At the time of the Tien An Men demonstration, the Mao government was mounting a literary campaign praising Ch'in Shih Hwang for his "revolutionary methods" of suppressing dissent, singling out for particular approval Ch'in's burning of books and his burying alive of dissenting scholars.

During this campaign the Maoist press frequently compared Ch'in Shih Hwang to Mao. It is an old tradition for political oppositions in China to attack powerful living leaders by indirection, criticizing some historical figure that the reader would have little difficulty identifying as a

The reverberations of the Tien An Men demonstrations did not end with the arrest of the last of the demonstrators. The Political Bureau went into emergency session. Two days later, on April 7, it issued a resolution that declared:

On the proposal of our great leader Chairman Mao, the Political Bureau unanimously agrees to dismiss Teng Hsiao-p'ing from all posts both inside and outside the Party while allowing him to keep his Party membership so as to see how he will behave in the future.[3]

The *People's Daily* on April 10 ran a featured editorial with a stinging attack on Teng, attributed to Mao:

Chairman Mao points out: "This person [Teng] does not grasp class struggle; he has never referred to this key link." "He knows nothing of Marxism-Leninism; he represents the bourgeoisie. He said he would 'never reverse the verdict' [try to restore capitalism]. It can't be counted on."[4]

In the week that followed the Tien An Men demonstration, tens of thousands of police and party cadres were mobilized for a house-to-house interrogation of Peking citizens to track down other participants. This led to hundreds of further arrests. In May the press reported a "public trial" in which two of the Tien An Men demonstrators were sentenced to death and three received terms of thirty years at hard labor. The others, whose number is unknown, were not tried. They remained in prison. In March 1977, just under a year later, wall posters in Peking announced that they had been released by the new government.

---

surrogate for someone in their own time. (After the purge of the "gang of four," they were accused of attacking Chou En-lai through this method, by publishing articles critical of the regime of the Duke of Chou, who lived two thousand years ago.)

The implication is that the Tien An Men poem is aimed not only at the Ch'in emperor but at his modern counterpart, Mao Tsetung. The official denunciation of the demonstration made this point explicitly: "The clamours of these counter-revolutionaries about combating 'Chin Shih Huang' . . . were out-and-out counter-revolutionary agitation in the same vein as the language used in Lin Piao's plan for a counter-revolutionary coup d'etat. . . . directing their spearhead at our great leader Chairman Mao" (*Peking Review*, April 9, 1976 [in *China Quarterly*, number 67, September 1976, p. 665]).

3. The "Gang of Four"

Throughout the summer of 1976 the Chinese press sought to prepare the country for the imminent death of Mao. The chairman stopped receiving foreign visitors, and photographs were published showing him more and more enfeebled. His death on September 9 became the occasion for an unprecedented outpouring of messages of condolence. Some people may have been surprised to find that many of these came from the leaders of world imperialism and from a host of military dictatorships around the globe. Foreign Maoists eulogized him in the most extravagant terms. The American *Monthly Review* wrote: "Mao was undoubtedly the greatest Marxist and revolutionary since Lenin, and history may in time rate him even higher. . . . Mao's greatness . . . lay precisely in his uncompromising commitment to revolution."[1] Henry Kissinger made a different assessment, praising Mao for having "created a durable relationship [with Washington] based on mutual confidence and perception of common interests."[2]

The mourners, as reported by Peking, included the shah of Iran, Indira Gandhi, President Marcos of the Philippines, the king of fascist Spain, and the military dictatorships of Indonesia, Brazil, Argentina, and Chile. The Pinochet junta in Chile, in fact, declared three days of national mourning with flags at half-mast.* Chile had been granted a loan upwards of $50 million by Peking in 1975.

Mao's body was hardly cold before the bureaucracy moved to

---

*The September 17, 1976, Hsinhua reported: "According to the 'National Radio' of Chile, Chilean Deputy Interior Minister Enrique Montero on September 10 declared September 12, 13 and 14 as days of official mourning for Chairman Mao Tsetung with flags on public buildings to be flown at half-mast."

smash his closest collaborators and repudiate as "fascist" policies previously associated with his name.

On October 6 or 7, four top party leaders, all Politburo
members, were placed under house arrest. These included Chiang
Ch'ing, Mao's widow; Wang Hung-wen, elevated by Mao to the
post of second party vice-chairman at the Tenth Party Congress
in 1973; Chang Ch'un-ch'iao, chief army political commissar and
Mao's principal lieutenant in the key industrial city of Shanghai
during the Cultural Revolution; and Yao Wen-yuan, the director
of China's communications media and the country's leading
journalistic exponent of Mao's thought since 1965. Mao's nephew,
Mao Yuan-hsin, and his daughter, Li Na, were also arrested.

On October 12 it was announced that Hua Kuo-feng had been
appointed chairman of the Chinese Communist Party, though
who appointed him remained a mystery, as the Central Committee had not met, and after purges and deaths only twelve
members remained of the twenty-one-member Politburo elected
three years before.

The capitalist press pictured the shift as a victory for the
"moderates," led by Hua Kuo-feng, over the "radicals," led by
Chiang Ch'ing. This terminology is misleading and obscures
more than it clarifies. Without question, there were policy issues
as well as personality clashes and power struggles involved in
the purge—or, as some would call it, the coup. (These issues are
taken up later, in the chapter on the "two-line struggle.") The
actual differences between the Mao faction and its opponents in
the hierarchy are quite complex and any examination of them is
compromised at the outset if it begins from the assumption that
Mao's people represented the Left and the Hua group the Right.

To begin with, these are not political formations of the Chinese
masses, or even of large factions in the CCP. There is no right to
form political tendencies within the CCP, no discussion of
conflicting programs, and no right of dissent. What the bourgeois
press calls the "radicals" was simply the central party leadership
after the Cultural Revolution, represented by Mao Tsetung and
his inner circle. This included Hua Kuo-feng until the time of
Mao's death, when Hua suddenly changed sides and ordered the
arrest of the other leaders of his own faction. The so-called
"moderates" are actually the remnants of the grouping in the
party leadership headed by Liu Shao-ch'i and Teng Hsiao-p'ing
before the Cultural Revolution. After 1966, these functionaries,
insofar as they were readmitted to important posts, existed in the
CCP only by renouncing their past views and capitulating to

Mao's personal authority. As a consequence, until Mao's death they could exist not as a genuine faction with a stated political program but only as a secret clique. The Mao group required the skills and experience of these disgraced officials, but at the same time held them in contempt and subjected them to continual humiliation of various kinds.

Teng Hsiao-p'ing, not Hua, was the real leader of these barely tolerated officials. This group did enjoy considerable backing from Chou En-lai, a supposition confirmed by the newly founded cult of Chou's personality promoted today by the new government, and by the extensive revelations since the arrest of the "gang of four" of persecutions of associates and friends of Chou En-lai during the entire period from 1966 to 1976.

The "radical-moderate" terminology was coined by the Western press in the last years of Mao's rule, largely on the basis of taking what the Mao leadership said about its defeated opponents in the party and identifying such people as "moderates," while taking what the Mao leadership said about itself and calling these figures "radicals." Not surprisingly, the "radicals" come out sounding superior and to the left of the "moderates."

As a result, "moderates" were supposed to be supporters of elitism, defenders of bureaucratic privilege, proponents of "law and order," and pragmatic industrializers. This actually is not too far from the truth. The attributes of the "radicals," however, stray into the realm of the Mao faction's own self-image: defenders of "pure communism," egalitarian wage levelers, proponents of mass political participation, and champions of revolutionary zeal.

These flattering appreciations are not grounded in the actual record of the Mao group in power. At most, these are almost unrecognizably idealized references to the fanaticism and mass ideological campaigns that were the distinctive hallmarks of the Maoist current. And as we come closer to the realities of Maoism in power, the use made of the "radical-moderate" terminology by the bourgeois press becomes still more disorienting. In addition to the virtues claimed by Maoism for itself, the term *radical* is used by the Western press to describe authoritarian abuses by the Maoists, as a means of discrediting radicalism.

It is better to dispense entirely with such unhelpful terminology and examine directly the record of the fallen "gang of four," which does not substantiate their claim to have represented a left wing in the CCP.

• *Chiang Ch'ing.* A former film actress, Chiang married Mao in 1939, but did not take an active public role in party affairs until 1964. In 1965 she was instrumental in dismissing almost all the leading actors, playwrights, and film directors on the Central Steering Committee for the film industry. In May 1966 she was appointed with Ch'en Po-ta, Mao's long-time private secretary, to head the Cultural Revolution Group.

She played a central part in eliminating Mao's factional opponents from the party leadership. She was one of the main mouthpieces for the democratic rhetoric the regime used to bring the Red Guard youth into action against Liu Shao-ch'i. Her most famous single act of the Cultural Revolution, however, was her September 5, 1967, speech announcing Mao's directive to the army to fire on "mass organizations or individuals" that refused to obey military orders. This was a decisive turning point in the crushing of the Red Guard student and worker movement that had gone beyond the regime's directives, beginning to raise its own demands and even to question Mao's wisdom.

After this, Chiang was China's cultural commissar, setting national policy on films, theater, literature, music, and, to a lesser degree, education. Her authoritarian role can be compared to that of Stalin's henchman Andrei Zhdanov in the impoverishment of Soviet culture in the late 1940s.

In 1960, some 1,300 periodicals were published in China. This was cut to 648 at the beginning of the Cultural Revolution, and by 1973 was slashed to about 50. Book publishing was reduced to the works of Mao, technical manuals, party political tracts, and a few novels, mostly written by committees, on the "two-line struggle." The film industry practically ceased to exist, producing nothing for years but a handful of documentaries and films of eight "model operas" personally rewritten by Chiang Ch'ing to make them more "political."

In education, the universities were closed for five years. They reopened in 1972, but with a greatly reduced student body. In the early 1960s, China's college enrollment stood at 900,000. At the beginning of 1976 it was only 500,000—and this in a nation of 900 million inhabitants! In addition, the length of study was cut from five years to three. And of these three, one was now devoted to manual labor and another to the study of current party documents and Mao's writings. The students were handpicked by the party for their political loyalty.

• *Wang Hung-wen.* The youngest of the central party leaders (he is in his early forties), Wang typified the qualities Mao's faction sought to cultivate in the Cultural Revolution. Until 1966, he was a member of the police force in a Shanghai cotton mill—which led the Western press to refer to him as a "worker." He was appointed to trade union leadership by the Maoist faction in Shanghai in October 1966. His principal distinction was his ruthlessness in breaking strikes by rank-and-file workers demanding pay increases and shorter hours.

• *Chang Ch'un-ch'iao*. Like Wang, Chang was a Shanghai party leader lifted up by the Cultural Revolution. Outranking Wang at the time, he played a central role in the defeat of Liu Shao-ch'i's local supporters, and then in the armed crushing of the independent workers' movement that arose to the left of the Maoist faction. After the creation of the "Shanghai Commune" in January 1967, Chang was instrumental in dismantling this relatively democratic body.

• *Yao Wen-yuan*. Peking's press czar since the Cultural Revolution, Yao first gained fame in Shanghai in 1965-66 as the most vituperative journalistic mouthpiece for the Mao faction in its campaign against Liu Shao-ch'i as a "capitalist agent." For a decade, Yao's articles were among the most rabid in their hostility to dissent of any kind and in promoting the cult of Mao's personality.

Ironically, it was just ten years before his fall that Yao himself launched the call to hunt down every critic of Mao's thought and "beat the wild dog to death."[3] Yao's patron having died, Hua Kuo-feng, trained in the same school, called on the party to "crush the heads of the four dogs."[4]

On the question of egalitarianism, the four "radicals" were no more left wing than those who ousted them, or those they themselves helped to discredit as "capitalist-roaders." Until purged, they continued to pocket salaries of some 400 yuan a month, thirteen times the pay of an unskilled worker. And the accusations raised against them after their downfall charged that their privileges extended far beyond their salaries. Whereas in 1976 Teng Hsiao-p'ing was accused of appropriating state funds to build a mansion on the outskirts of Peking, the allegations against Mao's stalwarts portrayed an even more extravagant misuse of state funds. A Hsinhua dispatch, for example, claimed:

Chiang Ching occupied two villas in the summer palace. Whenever she slept there, she demanded complete quietude. Planes at a nearby airport had to stop their sorties, production teams in the vicinity had to sign off their broadcasting and people had to be sent uphill to beat the woods to drive the birds away. Gardeners in the summer palace gritted their teeth and said: In the past Empress Dowager Tzu Hsi occupied the summer palace by herself. Now, whenever Chiang Ching and Company came, the whole park had to be closed. They ordered jasmine flower soup at one moment and jasmine flower rice at another. They ordered cold dishes served hot. Chiang Ching refused to eat watermelon served cold and ate only fresh-caught gold carps. After eating and drinking, they just walked away without paying the bills or paid only a nominal sum. When we asked them to pay at market price, they were offended and even scolded us.[5]

The *People's Daily* carried an article entitled "Maggots Undermining Socialism from Within," which alleged:

The "gang of four". . . . squandered public funds on extravagant, nonessential building projects and unscrupulously appropriated state funds and materials by hook or by crook to an almost inconceivable extent. For example, more than 23,000 yuan [US$11,960] was used as Wang Hungwen's living expenses during the four months of his stay in Shanghai last year. Chang Chun-chiao, too, spent money like dirt. Just for the pleasure of the "gang of four", he once approved, without authorization, the importation of more than 500 films with 15 million yuan on the pretext that there might be "something to learn artistically and technically from these films".[6]

Inasmuch as Chiang Ch'ing lived with Mao Tsetung, if these accounts are to be believed they are an exposure of the corrupt living standards not only of the "gang of four" but of the whole of the bureaucratic hierarchy. All the more so in that it was the Mao faction that paraded as the "radical" opponents of special privilege and frequently in the past published similar exposés of the graft and corruption of so-called capitalist-roaders. This kind of institutionalized stealing from the state treasury is especially glaring in a country where a skilled worker earns 60 yuan (US$31) a month. Wang Hung-wen's spending spree in Shanghai in 1975 came to thirty-two years' pay for a skilled worker.

As for the "moderates," there were no publicly voiced disagreements by any known official of the Chinese regime with any of its policies while Mao lived. Hua's own ascent is actually strikingly parallel to that of the ousted clique. He was virtually unknown to the majority of Chinese as late as the spring of 1976, when he was appointed premier. Five years before, he was an obscure provincial administrator in Hunan. At the time of his appointment as party chairman in October 1976, the Chinese press had not revealed his age, his birthplace, or his previous record in the party.

Hua's rise in the hierarchy came in 1971, when he was brought to Peking to help in the ouster of Lin Piao's followers in the party and army. On the basis of this experience he was elected to the

Politburo in 1973 and made chief of the secret police in 1975.

* * *

"Red flags are flying over the mountains and rivers, every-where in the motherland, and the faces of our eight hundred million people glow with joy. Hundreds of millions of people in all parts of our country have held mammoth demonstrations in the past few days. . . . They warmly celebrated Comrade Hua Kuo-feng's assuming the posts of chairman of the Central Committee of the Communist Party of China and chairman of the C.P.C. Central Committee Military Commission, hailed the great victory in smashing the plot of the antiparty clique of Wang Hung-wen, Chang Chun-chiao, Chiang Ching and Yao Wen-yuan to usurp party and state power, and denounced with great indignation the vile crimes of the 'Gang of Four'."—Peking *People's Daily* editorial, October 24, 1976.[7]

The aura of monolithic stability cultivated by the Peking regime in recent years was badly shaken by the purge. The world was frankly incredulous of the claims that some of the country's leading Maoists had for years and even decades participated in a secret conspiracy against Mao.

The still more preposterous allegation that Chiang Ch'ing was a "fascist" who sought the restoration of capitalism served only to discredit the new regime and to cast doubt on all of its public utterances that could not be independently verified.

Not a shred of evidence was offered, none of the accused were permitted to speak in their own behalf, and no one inside China's borders was allowed to ask embarrassing questions. The slogan of the moment, headlined in every Peking newspaper October 22, the day the purge was confirmed by the press, declared: "Rally most closely round the party Central Committee headed by Chairman Hua Kuo-feng and obey its orders in all actions." The "gang of four" was accorded the same treatment they had meted out to Liu Shao-ch'i, Lin Piao, and other top scapegoats of the winning faction.

Even if the government were to be taken at its word, the picture it painted of itself bore little resemblance to workers' democracy. A decade earlier, the head of state, the chief of the army general staff, the party general secretary, and the mayor of the capital city were stripped of their posts by the party chairman and accused of being spies for foreign capitalist governments. The chairman appointed a new heir, Lin Piao, who was hailed by demonstrations of cheering millions, only to die in a plane crash while fleeing to a hostile nation. He was posthumously accused of plotting the assassination of the leader.

After this, the disgraced "capitalist" party secretary, Teng Hsiao-p'ing, was returned to office, given top positions of military and state authority, then suddenly condemned again as a "bourgeois plotter." Finally, on the death of the leader, his wife and closest associates are discovered to have been conspiring all along to destroy the government they served.

These tales of venal intrigue, secret conspiracies, and treacherous betrayals would seem extraordinary even in a feudal court. How can they be explained in a society that has overthrown capitalism?

In fact, the stereotyped denunciations the CCP hierarchy uses to eliminate defeated groupings from its midst are not intended to convince or to be believed. Their purpose is to draw a curtain around the bureaucracy's inner circle, where decisions are made, and to exclude the party ranks and the mass of workers, peasants, and students from any role except that of rubber stamp for the victors.

There was nothing original or new in the methods used by Hua Kuo-feng to get rid of Chiang Ch'ing and the rest of the "gang of four." In general outline the procedure was perfected by Stalin in the mass purges of the 1930s. The Soviet bureaucracy then, like its Chinese counterpart today, sought not only to destroy its political opponents and the potential rivals of the supreme arbiter within the bureaucracy. It strove in the process to demoralize the workers. By choosing accusations that placed the purge victims outside the pale of political debate, and by compelling massive public endorsement of charges that everyone knew to be false, the regime conveyed a simple message: If even the mightiest could be felled by a word from the leader, and if no one dared raise a finger no matter how outrageous the allegations, what chance would an ordinary worker have who criticized the regime?

Mao effectively used these methods to maintain his grip on the Chinese party and state apparatus. He emphasized one aspect of the process that Stalin utilized only briefly in the 1930s: the calling of rallies and demonstrations and innumerable local meetings, all securely under party control, to validate his policies and give them the stamp of popular approval.

Many observers of People's China in the last decade or so have looked at the size of the crowds, the frequency of the "discussion" meetings, the apparent unanimity they produced, and concluded that Mao's policies were in some fundamental way more democratic and revolutionary than the Kremlin's. This impression was deepened by the fact that, unlike Stalin, Mao had headed his party during a great revolution. And there was also the Sino-Soviet rupture that surfaced in 1960, establishing China's independence from the Kremlin. This was often taken as synonymous with a break from Stalinism.

The latest purge is instructive in this regard. To trace its unfolding is to reveal more about the structure of China's bureaucratic caste than its authors intended.

A few days after the arrest of the four on October 6 or 7, rumors were set in circulation, accusing them variously of daring to put forward their own candidate in a secret Politburo election to choose Mao's successor as party chairman, of fabricating documents by Mao, and of plotting a coup against Hua Kuo-feng. Only later, in November, would some of the underlying policy disputes come to light.

The regime at first maintained a guarded silence on the purge, answering inquiries by Western diplomats and reporters with "no comment." But on October 15, a wall poster campaign began in major cities, denouncing the four by name.

The wall posters were unrestrained even by the standards of a regime that had seen the deposition and disgrace of its top leaders for a decade. Posters in Shanghai demanded: "Crush the heads of the four dogs" and "Crush and strangle the gang of four."[8]

Wall posters play a special role in the propaganda arsenal of the bureaucracy. They are part of the mystique of mass participation. They allow workers or students to let off steam about petty local issues in a press limited to one handwritten copy. They are a vehicle for budding functionaries to demonstrate to their superiors their facility in explaining the current party campaigns. They are an ideal means for anonymous denunciations of "troublemakers" in a factory, commune, or school.* And in a major purge, they permit the regime to float accusations that it is not yet prepared to officially endorse or explain.

No one can be sure in reading a wall poster if a particular

---

*Reactionary governments of every social basis, including the privileged bureaucratic castes that have fastened on workers' states, appropriate to themselves a popular or radical terminology that tries to allegation is definitely the official line or an exaggerated improvisation by some local party stalwart. Best of all, by beginning with a wall poster campaign the regime can present its subsequent action as taken by popular demand. Of course, wall posters that oppose the current line are quickly torn down and their authors arrested if they can be found.

Demonstrations against Chiang Ch'ing and her cronies came on the heels of the wall poster campaign. From the celebration atmosphere at these events, it was obvious that the "gang of four" had made many enemies outside as well as inside the ruling bureaucracy. Hua Kuo-feng had picked a popular target.

*   *   *

Chinese Stalinist jurisprudence operates in a different way from the norms of the early Soviet Union in Lenin's time, or even the procedures specified in the Chinese constitution. First comes the punishment, then the verdict, and only then are the charges revealed. The evidence is usually left out altogether.

In this case, four of the top party leaders were thrown in jail or placed under house arrest and stripped of their party and government posts. Then the masses were called into the streets to declare them guilty—before the government, the party, or the press had accused them of any specific crime.

Demonstrations—patently organized by the government and party—of tens of millions of people throughout the country had been going on for a week before a single official accusation was offered by the Chinese press. Finally on October 21, the country's leading newspaper, the Peking *People's Daily,* ran a front-page

---

camouflage the actual nature of their institutions. In France and Italy, old bourgeois parties parade under the name "Radical." In the semicolonies, the expectations of the masses are higher, and the capitalist class masquerades behind such high-sounding titles as National Revolutionary Front, People's Socialist Union, and so on.

In the USSR the "soviets" remain as institutions, stripped of their character as revolutionary workers' parliaments where contending political tendencies seek a mass following for their views. Similarly in China, the collective farms are labeled People's Communes and the agencies of local government are dubbed Revolutionary Committees. Neither the one nor the other resembles the revolutionary proletarian institution for which it is named. It would be confusing to coin new designations for these bodies and tedious to continually place them in quotation marks. The reader should keep in mind, however, that such things as communes and Revolutionary Committees in China are one and all different subdivisions of the bureaucratic apparatus of rule.

article under the headline "An Out-and-Out Old Capitulationist." This accused one of the four, Vice-premier Chang Ch'un-ch'iao, of being a "maggot" because of a book review he had written in 1936. Nothing he had done more recently was mentioned. And even here, Chang was referred to only by his pen name of forty years previous, known only to the initiates.

On October 22, two weeks after their arrest, the four were first mentioned by name in the Chinese press. Two slogans were launched. These read: "Warmly celebrate the appointment of Comrade Hua Kuo-feng as chairman of the Central Committee of the Communist Party of China and chairman of the C.P.C. Central Committee Military Commission!" and "Warmly celebrate the great victory in smashing the scheme of the 'gang of four' to usurp party and state power!"[9] This charge was the most detailed indictment and the sole evidence for the "guilty" verdict elicited from fifty million demonstrators.

Thereafter, hundreds of articles in the press from every corner of China dutifully reported that so and so many people from this and that walk of life had "warmly celebrated" these two events. The texts of hundreds of speeches and interviews were published, each affirming without the slightest elaboration or detail that the four had sought "to usurp party and state power" and stood condemned for their "towering crimes."

It is one thing to ask people to come into the streets to denounce hated officials for their actual and well-known abuses of power. It is quite another to ask millions of people to condemn someone for a supposed plot, allegedly carried out in secret, of which no details whatsoever are specified, much less proven. Here the verdict is demanded not only before the trial but even before the charges are made known.

Chiang Ch'ing was now at the receiving end of the system she had helped Mao to construct. When the Chinese working class and its allies overthrow their bureaucratic masters and win the fight for workers' democracy, they will have no reason to tell lies about their former oppressors or frame them up for things they did not do. The bureaucrats will undoubtedly get fairer treatment than they got from each other.

In the Moscow trials of the 1930s, Stalin invented elaborate accounts of the alleged conspiracies of his victims. These were torn to shreds and ridiculed before the world by Leon Trotsky, the chief defendant, in absentia. Trotsky amassed the documentary proof of the falsehood of the fabrications and dealt the Soviet bureaucracy a black eye it has never lived down.

Stalin's Chinese disciples learned a lesson from that experience. Unfortunately it was a Stalinist lesson: if you make the charge vague enough, it is harder to disprove. After the first unsubstantiated accusation of trying to "usurp power," the Chinese press filled in the dossier with wilder and wilder allegations that led further and further away from whatever it was that actually happened in early October.

One dispatch claimed:

Wang, Chang, Chiang and Yao are typical representatives of the bourgeoisie in the party. Their coming to power would mean the coming to power of the bourgeoisie, of revisionists and fascists and would mean the restoration of capitalism in China.[10]

"Worker-activists in theoretical study" from Shanghai factories, selected for special courses in Mao Tsetung Thought, offered this analysis to the Hsinhua reporter:

The anti-party clique of Wang, Chang, Chiang and Yao waved the banner of Marxism to wantonly oppose Marxism, and they stopped at no crime for all their fine words. They show their true colours before the mirror of invincible Marxism-Leninism-Mao Tsetung Thought, and have finally become something filthy and contemptible like dog's dung.[11]

Workers at the Taching model oil field accused the four of sabotaging the very campaigns of which they were the leaders over the past decade:

They wantonly interfered with and sabotaged the Great Proletarian Cultural Revolution, the movement to criticize Lin Piao and Confucius, and the great struggle to criticize Teng Hsiao-ping and repulse the right deviationist attempt to reverse correct verdicts which [was] initiated and led by Chairman Mao. They are the "maggots" worming their way into the revolutionary ranks . . . counterrevolutionaries who wear red hats to hide their black hearts.[12]

And finally, in case anything had been overlooked, "This counter-revolutionary clique perpetrated every conceivable crime and is unpardonably wicked."[13]

The Chinese leadership plainly operates on the old adage that any stick is good to beat a dog with. In October 1976, one of the "crimes" of Chiang Ch'ing was that she did not carry out the "great struggle to criticize Teng Hsiao-ping . . . initiated and led by Chairman Mao." A year later, her crime would be that she *did* criticize Teng. For those interested in historical truth there is not much to be had here. But it is probably worth noting that Hua's government, after they had gotten rid of the "gang of four," still said in 1976 that it was Mao himself who had ordered the purge of Teng.

The attacks on the vilified Politburo members soon turned more and more away from simple character assassination and came to involve a major policy realignment. The continued absence of democracy in China was confirmed by the closed nature of the discussion. What took place in November and December 1976 was not a debate over policy alternatives argued out openly before the masses and inviting their participation—much less a genuine democratic discussion in which the masses themselves controlled the press and had institutions such as workers' councils through which they could impose their will on their representatives. Instead, a secret discussion took place, evidently among the tiny group of Politburo members who were not in jail. The results of the debate were presented to the masses and the party as an accomplished fact. The previous line, identified with Mao Tsetung and the Cultural Revolution, became "counterrevolutionary."

Hua Kuo-feng and the veteran party and government bureaucrats who support him chose to carry out their switch in the name of Mao Tsetung Thought. Under this cover the new Chinese leadership admitted that the "politics in command" line of the Cultural Revolution had brought severe economic setbacks. In its place they began to revive many of the economic slogans associated with Liu Shao-ch'i and Teng Hsiao-p'ing. These had been long denounced in China and by Maoists throughout the world as the equivalent of "Soviet revisionism" and "capitalism."

The government also broadly hinted that now that Mao was gone his austerity program would be scrapped and there would be a liberalization in culture and the arts.

The veteran administrators, humiliated by Mao, were taking their revenge. They did not dare to act while Mao was alive, but now that he was gone they were "reversing the verdicts."

An article in the Peking *People's Daily* declared:

They [the four] were busy making intrigues and conspiracies and created splits, allowing only those who bowed before them to survive and casting out those who resisted them. *For years,* the "gang of four" have committed countless crimes against the party and the people, losing all popular support and becoming extremely isolated. The whole nation celebrates their downfall.[14] [Emphasis added.]

This clearly did not refer to a plot hatched after Mao's death or to acts during the last few months of his illness. Chinese readers would have little difficulty in getting the message that if the dominance of the "gang of four" went back *"for years,"* the gang must have had a fifth member—the chief protector of the four, Mao Tsetung.

This is the key to understanding the meaning of the purge. There was no separate "radical" faction while Mao was alive; there was only Mao's high command. This is the reason that Mao never publicly criticized any of the "gang of four," and they could be removed from office only after he had passed from the scene.* The four did occupy a special place in the party hierarchy that brought them the hatred not only of the masses but of many functionaries as well. Mao used them as a buffer between himself and the experienced administrators who remained at the end of the Cultural Revolution. The four played the part of what might be called a kitchen cabinet, composed of relatives, personal retainers, and young nonentities without any independent base in the party. Mao surrounded himself with such people.

None of the four had played any significant role in the party before 1966. Their rise was so abrupt that they were derisively referred to by Teng Hsiao-p'ing as "the helicopters." It was not surprising that without Mao's protection they were quickly disposed of.

It was not because the four differed with Mao that they were struck down, but because they were so completely identified with his line that they could not be preserved after a major policy shift.

The new government, after November 1976, did finally produce

---

*Peking has made a substantial effort to show that Mao was opposed to the fallen four, at least in the two or three years immediately prior to his death. To this end, a handful of quotations have been cited. What is striking in this, leaving aside whether the quotations are genuine or not, is that they were never made public while Mao was alive. Mao said harsher things about Teng Hsiao-p'ing and issued them to the press. Most of the criticisms of the four are on the level of "Don't form a gang of four," "Don't nitpick," "Chiang Ch'ing's speech was no good, don't distribute it," "Chiang Ch'ing has wild ambitions," etc.

Even taken at face value and out of their original context, nothing yet quoted implies a severing of political relations. At most they suggest that Mao was in the habit of making sharp remarks at the expense of his subordinates within his inner circle and that he was opposed to giving Chiang Ch'ing too much authority in the party.

its indictment of the "gang of four." But it was not an indictment for having tried to seize power in October 1976. It was a condemnation of what had been done with the power by those who held it for the previous decade, an indictment of that quintessence of Mao's thought, the Cultural Revolution.

Hua Kuo-feng, later joined by Teng Hsiao-p'ing, charged that the previous government had made a shambles of the economy through extolling empty revolutionary verbiage in place of serious work; that it had severely damaged China's industrialization plans through massive cutbacks in higher education and by persecuting scientists and technicians; that widespread discontent had been provoked by branding any rise in the people's living standards as bourgeois consumerism; that persecution of political and social nonconformism had reached such a scale as to demoralize workers and lower-level functionaries, who feared to take any initiative lest they be accused of counterrevolutionary behavior; and that culture and the arts had virtually ceased to exist in China under Mao.

The official press now depicted China after the Cultural Revolution as a police state run by incompetent zealots who burned books, rewarded ignorance, and punished the search for knowledge, even in fields far removed from politics in its normal meaning.

These revelations began abstractly enough, but by the fall of 1977 began to be backed up with a barrage of specific examples that presented a grim picture of the country where Mao had supposedly placed "proletarian politics" in command. And, while Mao remained enshrined as a national idol, the sum total of these revelations approached the level of Khrushchev's 1956 speech denouncing the crimes of Stalin.

The Chinese press since the fall of the "gang of four" has provided some picture of the actual content of the politics that Mao's faction placed in command. A "veteran steel worker" at the Maanshan Iron and Steel Company in Anhwei Province criticized the "gang of four" as follows:

Experience in the struggle has taught us the profound lesson that, by merely raising empty revolutionary slogans without a powerful socialist economic base, the dictatorship of the proletariat cannot be consolidated and modernization of China's agriculture, industry, national defence and science and technology and the lofty goal of communism can never be realized.[15]

A secretary of a workshop party branch was quoted as saying:

. . . the anti-party "gang of four" always tried to sabotage production by hook and by crook. They hurled such serious charges as "practising the theory of productive forces" and "not placing politics in command" at us.* Actually these bourgeois careerists and conspirators were unleashing poisonous arrows of idealism and metaphysics at us with the obvious aim of fooling the masses so that they could usurp party and state power.[16]

The Peking *People's Daily* generalized these accusations:

The "gang of four" advocated metaphysics frantically. With ulterior motives, they opposed revolution to production, politics to economy, class struggle to the struggle for production, and the dictatorship of the proletariat to socialist construction. They were against promoting production and construction. This would not only impede the expansion of production, but inevitably undermine the great cause of the proletarian revolution and the dictatorship of the proletariat. According to their logic,

---

*The so-called theory of productive forces was first announced in China during the Cultural Revolution. It was a criticism not only of Liu Shao-ch'i but of the whole Marxist theory of the priority of objective conditions and material reality. This, it was alleged, led to fatalism, a substitution of "production" for "class struggle," and the preservation—or restoration—of capitalism. Marx, Engels, and Lenin were not criticized by name, but the official texts attributed the theory to Karl Kautsky, Leon Trotsky, the "Soviet revisionists," and Liu Shao-ch'i.

Mao seems to have developed this notion at the time of the Sino-Soviet split as a means of overcoming—in the mind—the problem of constructing "socialism" solely within the borders of China. One of his most explicit statements of this view appears in his "Reading Notes on the Soviet Union's *Political Economy*," a criticism he wrote in the early 1960s of a Soviet textbook. This was published in China unofficially in 1967 during the Cultural Revolution. There Mao wrote:

"Lenin said: 'The transition from capitalism to socialism will be more difficult for a country the more backward it is.' This would seem incorrect today. Actually, the transition is less difficult the more backward an economy is, for the poorer they are the more people want revolution. In the capitalist countries of the West the number of people employed is comparatively high, and so is the wage level. Workers there have been deeply influenced by the bourgeoisie, and it would not appear to be all that easy to carry through a socialist transformation. And since the degree of mechanization is high, the major problem after a successful revolution would not be advancing mechanization but transforming the people." ("Mao on Soviet Economics and Other Subjects," *Monthly Review* [New York], September 1977, p. 7.) What Mao leaves out here, of course, is precisely the effect of poverty and the absence of advanced technology in generating a privileged bureaucracy after the overthrow of capitalist rule. History endorses Lenin on this question and not Mao Tsetung.

when the "satellites go up into the sky", the red flag would inevitably "trail in the dust": If the 800 million people want to "make revolution", they should feed themselves only with northwest wind.[17]

It is true that this is not a debate in the ordinary sense of the word. The statistics of the actual performance of the Chinese economy are missing, and the faction in power conducts a strident monologue in which actual policy issues are at best clouded. But it is plain enough that important differences in economic priorities, not just in ideological slogans, played a central part in the factional struggle between Mao and his rivals. That this dispute was not just over future perspectives was confirmed when, in October 1977, Minister of Economics Yu Ch'iu-li reported to a meeting of the standing Committee of the Fourth National People's Congress that there had been "grave damage to the national economy" in the years between the Cultural Revolution and Mao's death.[18]

There is no doubt that other issues besides economic production figure in the ten-year factional war in the CCP hierarchy. Some of these will be touched on later. There is also the problem of how much to believe of what Peking now says about the previous government. Much of this is patently exaggerated, or simply invented to serve factional ends. But a great deal can be independently confirmed; if by no other means, then by the dramatic flip-flops in the regime's stated priorities paralleling the rise, fall, and final reemergence of Teng Hsiao-p'ing.

At the outset of the Cultural Revolution in 1966, Mao proclaimed the failure of the "Soviet model" in China, and drove from the party leadership those administrators most closely associated with Moscow's planning methods and procedures. The fallen officials in their turn, now restored to power, are passing judgment on what could be called the "Maoist model" of economic development. The claims of both sides—as well as the objective needs of China's development—must be examined against the actual experience of China's nationalized economy. Part II attempts to draw such a preliminary balance sheet.

Part II

The Economy

4. Planned Economy and Socialism

A democratically planned economy has immense inherent advantages over the anarchy of capitalism. No usable goods need remain unsold in warehouses as long as there are people who need them. Capital—in this case state finances—is not withheld from investment in new productive capacity because of drops in the profit rate. The government has the capacity to rapidly shift both labor and factories to meet pressing or unexpected needs.

This is all summed up in the formula: Production for need and not for profit. There are many ramifications of such a basic difference. In a privately owned economy, capital must expand continually or the individual capitals that make it up will be eliminated in competition. Here is the root of colonialism, imperialism, and modern war. This inherent drive for markets and fields of investment is eliminated along with the private ownership of the means of production. For all the retrograde features of the Stalinist regimes of China or the Soviet Union, neither is inherently expansionist in the way that the governments of the United States, Western Europe, and Japan must be to preserve their economic system.

Under capitalism, because of the determining weight of the paying market, the unequal distribution of income that flows from private property leads to tremendous waste. There exist, side by side, extremes of poverty and fabulous wealth. Significant social resources are devoted to producing luxury goods consumed by only a tiny percentage of the population, while basic necessities may be in short supply or be overpriced through the manipulations of monopoly corporations.

Finally, under capitalism large numbers of people must be condemned to unemployment while still others are employed in occupations such as advertising, public relations, domestic service, war production, etc., which detract from society's capacity to fulfill real needs. On top of this comes the inevitable business cycle, periodically idling large sections of the productive plant and placing additional burdens on working people.

Social welfare measures appear under capitalism as a deduction from profits either in the form of corporate taxes, or, what is the same thing, in the form of higher wages so that the taxes can be taken from workers' pay. Thus they are strongly resisted by both the corporations and their government.

Under a planned economy these features are either eliminated outright, or, even under Stalinism, greatly attenuated. There is no longer a reserve army of the unemployed—or a permanent mass of underemployed—which in underdeveloped capitalist countries constitutes an enormous portion of the population. Individual labor is directly recognized as a contribution to social labor, and the state guarantees at least a minimum wage to everyone and finds them work to do.

"Profit" is at most an accounting device used to compare the costs of production with the social income generated by the product. No factory, if it produces something actually needed by people, can go out of business simply because its books do not register a "profit." Similarly, welfare measures do not threaten the economic survival of the basic production units of society, since this is not determined by competition on the market and is not affected, except in its rate of growth, by the withdrawal of funds to use for health, education, and welfare.

These advances over capitalism are progressive and have to be preserved, defended, and expanded. They must be the starting point of any serious balance sheet of the economic accomplishments of the Chinese socialist revolution.

At the same time, to say that the Chinese revolution has abolished capitalism is not the same thing as saying that it has, under the CCP, succeeded in creating a genuine socialist society, or even that it has embarked on a course that can successfully lead to socialism.

For Marx, a planned economy was conceived first and foremost as an international economy, based on a world division of labor. The narrow nationalism of the Stalinists has done much to obscure this fundamental idea of socialism, but it remains the essential step that must be taken if poverty and oppression are to be eliminated on this planet.

Maoist "self-reliance" is ultimately a formula for trying to pull oneself up by one's own bootstraps. Growth takes place, of course, but the imperialist centers have such a massive headstart in social wealth, urbanization, technology, scientific training, general culture—that is, above all, in the *proletarianization* of the population, that even a planned economy in an isolated backward country would require virtually a historical epoch to duplicate on its own the progress of the advanced countries.

The result is not, as some would have it, that socialism, however slowly, is being built, but without democracy. Such a view reduces the problem of socialism to a few cosmetic reforms— the grafting of a human face onto the framework built by the Stalinists. This is not the case. The pace at which economic construction is actually proceeding in the non-European workers' states, if continued in national isolation, will condemn their populations not merely to a lifetime but to generations of low-grade material existence.

At this point the reader may object on two counts. First, hasn't Chinese economic development been relatively rapid, particularly in social welfare and health measures? Doesn't this invalidate the need to insist on an international economic division of labor, at least to achieve a level of prosperity comparable to the advanced capitalist countries? Second, what alternative does the Chinese leadership really have? After all, no one is offering them any aid; and there *hasn't* been any successful socialist revolution in an advanced country.

The following four chapters attempt to answer the first objection through a balance sheet on Chinese economic development under Mao, breaking this down by industrial growth, agricultural production correlated to population increase, and finally, the overall rate of increase in social wealth.

The second question—what alternative does Peking have?—is in some respects more complex. Any workers' government in China would be compelled to ensure the livelihood of the Chinese people on the basis of the country's own internal resources during the period—which we are still in—of preparation for the extension of the world revolution. But there is the rub. Does Peking pursue policies that facilitate the development of socialist revolutions elsewhere?

Chapter 9 seeks the roots of China's foreign policy in the social physiognomy of the privileged bureaucracy that makes it, no less than the capitalist rulers of the West, an opponent of further overturns of capitalism. And the course of the bureaucracy in world politics is traced in Chapter 10.

5. Achievements
of the Chinese Revolution

The achievements of any society, particularly one undergoing dramatic reorganization and change, must be weighed by two scales: first, by what came before; and second, by the objective needs that must be met.

China's immediate past, the century before its socialist revolution, was among the darkest times in its history. Harold Isaacs writes:

> The invasion of the village by commercial capital and cheap manufactured commodities put an end to the peasant's old self-sufficiency. But because the country remained backward in communications and production techniques, the peasant could not adapt himself to the change. He was simply ruined by it. He had to produce for sale in order to exist, yet the smallness of his land and the primitive character of his farming made it difficult, if not impossible, for him to do this with much success. He not only could not produce enough to provide him with a surplus, but had to go into debt for fertilizer, for food to tide him over until harvesttime, for seed, for the rental and use of implements. For these he mortgaged away not only his crop but his land, at rates of interest never lower than 30 percent and more often 60, 70, 80 percent and even higher. The crushing burden of taxes and the rapacious extortions of the militarists who came to rule over him drove the peasant more deeply into debt each successive year and placed him and his land at the mercy of the usurer and the tax collector.[1]

The effects of this impoverishment on the health and life of the rural population may be imagined. Dr. Joshua S. Horn, who served as a surgeon in China for fifteen years after the revolution, gave this description of what existed before:

> Poverty and ignorance were reflected in a complete lack of sanitation as a result of which fly and water-borne diseases such as typhoid, cholera, dysentery, took a heavy toll. Worm infestation was practically universal,

for untreated human and animal manure was the main and essential soil fertilizer. The people lived on the fringe of starvation and this so lowered their resistance to disease that epidemics carried off thousands every year. The average life expectancy in China in 1935 was stated to be about twenty-eight years.[2]

With this as a starting point, the gains in China are truly impressive, in a whole range of areas. The new regime encouraged mass efforts to eliminate such age-old scourges as epidemic disease, famine caused by unequal distribution of basic foodstuffs, illiteracy, prostitution, forced marriage of women and young girls, and many other abuses of the old society. Some of these achievements are summarized by John G. Gurley in his book *China's Economy and the Maoist Strategy:*

> The basic, overriding economic fact about China is that for twenty years it has fed, clothed, and housed everyone, has kept them healthy, and has educated most. Millions have not starved; sidewalks and streets have not been covered with multitudes of sleeping, begging, hungry, and illiterate human beings; millions are not disease-ridden. To find such deplorable conditions, one does not look to China these days but, rather, to India, Pakistan, and almost anywhere else in the underdeveloped world. . . .
>
>   . . . On top of this, there have been large gains in the supplies of eggs, vegetables, fruits, poultry, fish, and meat. . . . The Chinese are in a much better position now than ever before to ward off natural disasters, as there has been significant progress in irrigation, flood control, and water conservation. The use of chemical fertilizers is increasing rapidly, the volume now being over ten times that of the early 1950s; there have been substantial gains in the output of tractors, pumps, and other farm implements; and much progress has been made in the control of plant disease and in crop breeding.[3]

The most dramatic results have been in public health, primary education, and the supply of elementary foodstuffs, clothing, housing, and work to the whole of the population. To make these advances China also had to eliminate monetary inflation, so destructive to the standard of living of working people in all semicolonial capitalist countries. One report on public health in China tells us:

> Massive campaigns of inoculation and public health education, intensification of medical training, and widely distributed health services have virtually wiped out diseases that were rampant in the past—diphtheria, whooping cough, tetanus, smallpox, polio, cholera, tuberculosis—even syphilis. The Chinese, like ourselves, now most commonly die of cancer

and heart disease, a sign of great progress since encounter with these killers generally comes in advanced years.[4]

The scope of these accomplishments is difficult to grasp at once. Each of these diseases affected tremendous numbers before the revolution. A medical examination at one Peking university in 1948, for example, revealed that 18.2 percent of the students suffered from active cases of tuberculosis.[5]

In 1947 there were only 66,000 hospital beds in the whole country. By 1956 this had been increased to 262,000.[6] More recent figures have not been published, but it is reasonable to believe that this number has increased in the past twenty years.

Parasitic infestations—hookworm, malaria, schistosomiasis, kala-azar, and filariasis—which were rampant in the countryside, were also brought under control by the early 1960s.

The major campaign to provide adequate medical services for the rural areas is something new in China, where the peasants previously lived and died without ever seeing a doctor. It has been a two-pronged effort, involving the training of tens of thousands of "barefoot doctors," paramedics with limited knowledge but still able to administer programs that had previously been lacking; plus having fully trained physicians spend some time in rural communes.

Some of the accounts of this program are very moving, telling us both of the strides that have been taken, and the extreme poverty of the Chinese countryside that remains even today. Dr. Joshua Horn recounts a discussion with a Chinese doctor who was part of such a team with him in a village in northern Hopei province in 1965:

. . . I expected that the process of adjustment from the soft city life to the hard life of the villages would be difficult. . . . But I was often surprised to see how quickly my colleagues settled down. Within a few short weeks most of them were enjoying enormous meals of coarse grain which they would never have looked at in Peking, participating enthusiastically in heavy manual labour and feeling thoroughly at home with the peasants. I expressed my surprise to a rather pampered young woman doctor whose airs and graces had earned her the doubtful title of "Shanghai miss". She said, "Yes—I'm surprised too. Before I came down here I thought I'd never be able to live on millet. It's so hard and my stomach has always been delicate. But funnily enough it seems to agree with me. For the first few weeks, life here was really very difficult. The brick kangs [fire-heated traditional sleeping platforms] were terribly hard to sleep on, I had a horror of lice, the latrines disgusted me and I hated the idea of eating from the same bowl as the peasants. Now I have got used to all these things. I sleep much more soundly than in Peking, lice are nothing to be afraid of and the peasants are so kind and generous that I feel ashamed of my squeamishness. After all, why should I be so choosy? These peasants work from dawn to dusk almost every day of the year producing food for all of us."[7]

It is difficult to quantify the effect on people's lives of these measures. We get an impression from Canadian economist Barry Richman, who concluded from his studies that in 1966 an average citizen in China "could expect to live twelve to sixteen years longer" than before the revolution.[8]

Two of the most common measures of general social progress are infant mortality and literacy. We have seen some of the successes of the Chinese government in improving public health. Despite the setbacks to higher education in the post-Cultural Revolution years, the government has continued to promote elementary education and the long-standing efforts to teach illiterate adults to read and write.

The results in these areas are difficult to assess, as it is more than seventeen years since any statistics have been published. When Western economists have tried to make estimates on the basis of the fragmentary data available, these have often been very favorable to China. Table 1 provides a comparison of infant mortality rates and literacy in China with those in several other Asian countries, as well as with the U.S. and the Soviet Union.

These figures show that for health care and primary education, China has reached the levels of the advanced countries and is no longer in the same category as most of the semicolonial nations.

In the following chapters we will examine the development of industry and food production. But one further social achievement of the Chinese revolution should be taken up here. Despite the bureaucracy and all of its abuses, the land and the factories are no longer the private property of a capitalist class. This means that collective work for their improvement can be undertaken and is not intrinsically stifled from the outset because these are someone else's private property.

Every visitor to the Chinese countryside brings back their own stories of the initiative and cooperative labors of the peasantry in irrigation works, soil reclamation, construction, and a host of other beneficial projects that would not have been done or could not have been done on the same scale before the revolution. One account, which could be multiplied manyfold, is that of an old peasant from a poor commune in north China shortly before the

TABLE 1

Infant Mortality and Literacy Rates in China, Selected Asian Countries, the United States, and the USSR*

	Infant mortality (per 1,000)	% literate adults
China	20	96
Bangladesh	130	35
Burma	100	67
India	139	36
Indonesia	125	56
Iran	40	40
Malaysia	26	60
Pakistan	124	25
Philippines	68	72
Sri Lanka	45	70
Thailand	23	80
United States	18	98
USSR	26	98

*Asia 1977 Yearbook (Hong Kong: Far Eastern Economic Review, 1977), p. 14.

Cultural Revolution. He had been a patient of Dr. Joshua Horn after a serious injury had required that he go to Peking for treatment. Horn later visited "Old Zhang" at his commune:

The thin mountain air parched my lips and the sun reflected from the stone-clad mountain sides dazzled my eyes. For all his recent injury and for all his fifty years of hard toil, Old Zhang, deeply suntanned and sprouting a stubbly little beard, was as nimble as a mountain goat and I had difficulty in keeping up with him. . . . On the way down he pointed out landmarks in the village below.

"See those houses with tiled roofs down there?" he said. "We built those last year. They may not look very grand to you since you came from London, one of the great cities of the world. But we like them very much. The heavy roofs keep out the summer heat and the winter cold. During the past twelve years we have built an extra four rooms per family.

"That building over there is our new school. In the old days the likes of us never had the faintest possibility of going to school—not even to see what it was like. I know, because when I was a kid I was terribly curious to see what went on in school and one day I smuggled myself in. But they found me and kicked me out. They told me I was a disgrace because I had brought fleas into the school.

"Now all the children in the Commune aged eight and over go to school. If a child is sick for any length of time, we have a special teacher who goes to his home to teach him there. This brigade has two primary schools and one half work/half study middle school. We even have four students at the University, including my eldest boy who is studying geology in Changsha."[9]

There is something different taking place here from life in poor countries that remain under capitalism. Energies have been released that would have no productive outlet in a country such as India or Indonesia. That is the brighter part of the picture of China today.

6. China's Industrial Growth

There are many yardsticks for judging economic growth. The most reliable and measurable elements are the output of material goods such as steel or cement over a period of years. Less definite but no less important are estimates of Gross National Product, workers' wages, and the average increase in industrial productivity.

To begin, let us take an estimate of overall industrial growth made by John Gurley. After listing the accomplishments cited in the previous chapter, Gurley added:

> While all these gains were being made, the Chinese were devoting an unusually large amount of resources to industrial output. China's industrial production has risen on the average by at least 11 percent per year since 1950, which is an exceptionally high growth rate for an underdeveloped country.[1]

To this estimate we can add Chou En-lai's report to the Fourth National People's Congress in January 1975, that industrial growth had been in the range of 11 percent per year for the decade 1964-74.[2]

The existing economic evidence bears out both these claims. On its face this is an exceptional record, and a sustained one. Here, however, we begin to run into some difficulties.

For years, every major speech emanating from Peking has summed up its report on the Chinese economy with the ritualistic words, "the situation is excellent." We will return to how Gurley and Chou arrived at their figures. First, let us give the floor to China's current minister of economics, Vice-Premier Yu Ch'iu-li.

Shortly after the purge of the "gang of four," the Chinese press began to strike a new note on the state of the economy, urging workers to "make up for the losses in time and material wealth" caused by "sabotage" from the highest levels of the government. It was some time before any details were made public of the conditions Mao had bequeathed to his successors. A series of national conferences were held. These included a conference to learn from Tachai, a model agricultural production brigade; a Central Work Conference; a National Conference on Railway Work; a National Planning Conference; a Learn-From-Taching (the model oil field) Conference; a plenum of the Central Committee; the Eleventh Party Congress in August 1977; and finally a meeting of the Standing Committee of the Fourth National People's Congress in October 1977.

At this last gathering, Yu Ch'iu-li reported that there had been "grave damage to the national economy," and "there was a stagnation in industrial and agricultural production and a decline in the output of a number of industrial products." The arrest of the Mao faction leaders, he said, had come just in time to avert "the collapse of our national economy." Following are some of the main points made by Yu:

. . . Bad elements usurped power in some localities and units. Capitalist forces became rampant there. Corruption and graft, theft, speculation and profiteering were rife and socialist ownership was undermined.

The state revenue from January to September [1977] was 7.8 percent over the same period of 1976. This put to an end several years of failure to fulfill state quotas.

. . . In the Anshan Iron and Steel Company, China's largest, the workers and staff were so harshly oppressed by the gang's sworn follower in Liaoning and his antiparty faction that they could not lift their heads. Production stagnated for a long time; accidents were frequent and equipment was seriously damaged. . . .

Szechwan, known as a "land of heavenly gifts", was badly affected by the "gang of four" over the past few years. It had been reduced from a grain supplier to a grain deficient province and industrial production plummeted. . . .

I would like to add here that, owing to grave interference and sabotage by the "gang of four", there are still many problems in economy. Some of the proportional relations in the national economy and the normal order of the socialist economy are deranged and these problems cannot be solved within the short space of one year, and the many shortcomings in our concrete work have added to the difficulties in developing the national economy. Firstly, the growth of agriculture and light industry falls short of demand for the country's construction and the people's life; secondly, the development of the fuel and power industries and the primary goods industry is not keeping pace with the growth of the whole national economy; thirdly, consolidation of economic management and the management of enterprises has just begun, and no significant improvement has yet been made as regards the poor quality of products, big consumption of material, low labour productivity, high production cost and the tying-up of too much funds, which continue in some of our enterprises. And lastly, there are some problems in the people's life.[3]

Several places here Yu Ch'iu-li refers to damage done over "several years," "a long time," "the past few years," etc. It seems hard to avoid the conclusion that he is drawing a balance sheet on the economic innovations of the Cultural Revolution as a whole.

How do we reconcile Vice-Premier Yu's revelations with the more flattering statistics of John Gurley and Chou En-lai? The answer is that Chinese industrial development under Maoism has proceeded in dramatic fits and starts. It has gone through short spurts of exceptionally rapid development, followed by periods of near chaos and decline. To make economic sense of long-term averages such as Gurley and Chou offer, they must be broken down into particular periods and into specific achievements in production.

A comprehensive picture of what has actually been produced is summed up in Table 2. Many of the totals are impressive. But they do not show regular and sustained economic growth. Rather the table reveals erratic ups and downs. Moreover, the pace of growth is significantly greater in the early years of the People's Republic and, apart from the sheer disaster in the early 1960s after the Great Leap Forward, slows down significantly in the 1970s.

To speak of an average growth rate of 11 percent a year since 1950 tells us something, but is also misleading, as this means leveling a number of highly disparate growth rates in different periods.

According to Canadian economist Barry Richman:

In terms of overall industrial growth, Red China achieved an average annual rate of over 20. percent during 1953-59, and about 15 or 16 percent during 1953-57.[4]

By way of comparison, he adds:

India's annual average rate of industrial growth in the 1950's was no more than 6 percent; for Russia it was roughly 9.5 percent, for the United States less than 4 percent, but for Japan it was over 13 percent. The Soviet Union achieved a rate of roughly 12 percent—some industrial-production indexes place it as low as 9.9 percent and as high as 14.2

TABLE 2

Industrial Production in China, Selected Years, 1952-1976*

	Units	1952	1957	1960	1961	1965	1970	1973	1976
Steel	Million metric tons	1.4	5.4	18.7	8.0	12.5	17.8	25.5	21.0
Coal	"	66.5	130.7	280.0	170.0	220.0	310.0	377.0	445.0
Crude oil	"	0.4	1.5	5.5	5.3	10.8	28.5	54.5	84.0
Chemical fertilizer	"	0.2	0.8	2.5	1.8	7.5	14.0	24.8	28.0
Cement	"	2.9	6.9	12.0	8.0	14.8	19.8	29.9	37.3**
Electric power	Billion kilowatt hours	7.3	19.3	47.0	31.0	42.0	72.0	101.0	130.0
Cotton cloth	Billion linear meters	3.8	5.1	4.9	3.3	6.4	7.5	7.6	7.6**

*Figures for 1952 to 1973 are from *Far Eastern Economic Review* (Hong Kong), October 3, 1975. In turn, its figures for 1952-60 are official Peking government statistics taken from the standard source, the State Statistical Bureau pamphlet *Ten Great Years: Statistics of the Economic and Cultural Achievements of the People's Republic of China* (Peking: Foreign Languages Press, 1960). Since Peking did not publish many statistics between 1960 and 1970, figures for those years from any source must be regarded as approximations. The post-1970 figures are in line with individual production totals issued occasionally by Peking. The source for the 1976 totals is the October 7, 1977, *Far Eastern Economic Review.* (**)Cement and cotton cloth figures for 1976 are not available; figures given are for 1975. The source is *Asia 1977 Yearbook* (Hong Kong: Far Eastern Economic Review, 1977), p. 159.

percent—during the 1927/28-1937/38 period—that is, during her first two five-year plans.[5]

Arthur G. Ashbrook, Jr., an American economist who has specialized in the economy of China, places China's industrial growth in the 1950s even higher, at 22.3 percent a year for the entire period 1950-57.[6]

*   *   *

Chou En-lai's 1975 report, then, confirmed that China's industrial growth rate in the 1960s and 1970s was only half of what it had been in the 1950s. What had changed in the interim? One factor is the low starting point. Beginning with practically nothing, even a small step will produce large percentage changes. Later, when the total volume of output is greater, the same absolute increase will add a smaller percentage of the whole. This effect certainly operated in figures for crude oil and chemical fertilizer, which were produced in only infinitesimal quantities in China before the revolution. Likewise, this seriously affects figures for steel output until about 1955 or 1956, when enough basic plants had been put into operation to make it an integral part of the economy.

Still, there are other factors. One is the initial enthusiasm of the masses on seeing the overthrow of the hated Chiang Kai-shek regime. This went a long way, and for a number of years, in counterbalancing the lack of genuine mass participation in government or planning.

Another factor was Soviet aid. In absolute terms, this was doled out stingily by Stalin and his successors, but it showed the impact even a limited international division of labor and sharing of technology can have in rapidly modernizing a poor country. The converse was also true: when Khrushchev abruptly halted Soviet aid to China in 1960 it dealt the Chinese economy a severe blow. In many cases, Russian technicians were required to operate highly technical plants, and these had to shut down until Chinese scientists had mastered the techniques.

In the Great Leap Forward of 1958-60 (which will be discussed more fully in Chapter 11) Mao Tsetung sought to use a mass mobilization of China's labor force to dramatically surpass the already high growth rates of the mid-1950s. Instead, the ambitious plan failed—machines, and men and women, were pushed to the breaking point to fulfill unrealistic quotas; transport and supply systems collapsed; and finally both industrial and agricultural production came almost to a standstill. In the process, the conditions that made the rapid growth of the 1950s possible were dissipated and such growth rates were never matched again.

By the time of Chou En-lai's report at the beginning of 1975 he was not concerned about admitting that China's industrial development had slowed to half its 1950s speed, but about reassuring the Chinese masses that industry was really back on its feet and doing better than in the early 1960s.

There is one evident distortion in Chou's figures, however. As Table 2 indicates, even by 1965 Chinese industrial output had not pulled back up to the 1960 levels in a number of important sectors. Thus when Chou spoke of an 11 percent a year growth rate in industry, some of this must be counted as regaining ground that had been lost during the Great Leap Forward, and should therefore be at a higher rate than growth measured from a more normal base year.

The Maoists tend to discount the Great Leap debacle as some kind of natural calamity, caused solely by bad weather and the withdrawal of Soviet aid. Undoubtedly these factors affected agricultural and industrial output considerably. But in the intraparty dispute many leaders placed the principal blame for the collapse on Mao's voluntarist and arbitrary campaign.*

If we take a longer span than Chou does, and if we do not start out with the years of recovery, we can see what was actually lost. Table 3 does this, showing the output totals for the sixteen years from 1960 to 1976, for seven key indicators, and charting the long-term annual growth rate for each. It bears little resemblance to an 11 percent annual industrial growth rate.

With the exception of crude oil and chemical fertilizer, industrial growth for more than half of the lifetime of the People's Republic of China has achieved an annual cumulative rate of between 3 and 6 percent, with steel falling into long-term stagnation.

---

*After his purge in the Cultural Revolution some years later, China's head of state, Liu Shao-ch'i, was accused of saying that on his inspection tours of Hunan province, peasants had told him that the setbacks in food production were "70 per cent" the result of "man-made disasters." Liu was charged with having concluded that "the people's communes were premature," and the Great Leap Forward "not worthwhile" ("Chronicle of Liu Shao-ch'i's Crimes Against the Party, Socialism and Mao Tse-tung's Thought," cited in Philip Bridgham, "Factionalism in the Central Committee" in John Wilson Lewis [ed.], *Party Leadership and Revolutionary Power in China* [Cambridge: Cambridge University Press, 1970], p. 224).

TABLE 3

Sixteen Year Growth of Selected Industrial Indicators 1960-1976*

	Units	Total output 1960	Total output 1976	Average annual % of growth
Steel	Million met. tons	18.7	21.0	0.8
Coal	"	280.0	445.0	2.9
Crude oil	"	5.5	84.0	18.6
Chemical fertilizer	"	2.5	28.0	16.3
Cement	"	12.0	37.3	7.9**
Electric power	Billion kilowatt hours	47.0	130.0	6.6
Cotton cloth	Billion linear meters	4.9	7.6	3.4**

*Figures for 1960, *Far Eastern Economic Review,* October 3 1975. For 1976, ibid., October 7, 1977. (**)Figures for cement and cotton cloth are not available for 1976; those given are for 1975, taken from *Asia 1977 Yearbook* (Hong Kong: Far Eastern Economic Review, 1977), p. 159.

TABLE 4

Growth of Selected Industrial Indicators
for the Years 1970-76*

	Units	Total output 1970	1976	Average annual % of growth
Steel	Million met. tons	17.8	21.0	2.8
Coal	"	310.0	445.0	6.2
Crude oil	"	28.5	84.0	19.7
Chemical fertilizer	"	14.0	28.0	12.2
Electric power	Billion kilowatt hours	72.0	130.0	10.3
Cotton cloth	Billion linear meters	7.5	7.6	0.3**

*Figures for 1970, *Far Eastern Economic Review,* October 3, 1975. For 1976, ibid., October 7, 1977. (**) Figure for cotton cloth is not available for 1976; figure given is for 1975, taken from *Asia 1977 Yearbook* (Hong Kong: Far Eastern Economic Review, 1977), p. 159.

What this really measures, of course, is not any actual year-by-year growth rate. It is a combined "average" of the early 1960s, when there was deepgoing economic dislocation, and a decade of painful recovery and the beginnings of new growth. What is most striking is the costs of Stalinism for the people of China in a decade of minimal economic progress.

Finally, it can be argued that the figures for 1960 were artificially inflated by the Chinese government and that this can throw off the sixteen-year comparison. This is plausible, but would not change things significantly. Pretty much the same results can be obtained without using the Great Leap statistics at all. If total increase in industrial output from 1950 to, say, 1975, averages out to 11 percent a year, as John Gurley has shown; and if the first ten years proceeded at about a 22 percent per year increase, the most recent fifteen years must have grown at barely 4 percent a year. Since we know that the last ten have been at a higher rate than that, there is only one possible conclusion. In the early 1960s, the economic debacle was so great that China was thrown back to levels of the early 1950s and had to start all over again. And the climb back over lost ground was at a much slower pace than the first time around.

But what of the most recent period? Has a new, post–Great Leap and post–Cultural Revolution growth rate solidified? A tentative answer can be gained from Table 4, which views the years 1970-1976. This is a long enough period to at least make possible tentative conclusions. The period should be a particularly favorable one for the Chinese government, because it begins after the disruptions of the Cultural Revolution and it eliminates the distorting factor in counting from 1964, as the recovery following the Great Leap was complete by 1970.

One thing is immediately apparent. The rate of growth for these sectors is too low, and frequently far too low, to represent an 11 percent per year overall industrial growth.

Steel in particular—once getting the plant that had been constructed in the 1950s back into full operation—has moved upward very little since. The 1976 figures are actually a decline, not an all-time high. From 17.8 million tons in 1970 production reached 25.5 million in 1973. In 1974 it fell back to 23.8 million. In 1975 the 1973 figure was almost matched, but plummeted again in 1976.[7]

The best available estimates of China's 1977 steel production put it at about 24 million tons, still below the output of 1973.[8]

Steel is not just one item among many. A whole range of

industrial activities depend on a guaranteed supply of steel if they, in turn, are to grow. The Chinese government does not issue any hard figures, for example, on such directly related industries as building construction, including housing; railroad building; machine-tool manufacture; shipbuilding; automobiles, trucks, farm implements, and tractors, etc. The stagnation in steel must have affected these sectors as well.

Cotton cloth is another product whose output has stagnated over a number of years. In 1955 China produced 4.4 billion linear meters (BLM) of cloth. This grew to 7.5 BLM in 1970, a growth rate of about 3.5 percent a year. But after that, it hit 7.2 in 1971, 7.3 in 1972, reaching 7.6 in 1973, where it stayed for the next two years. There are no figures available for 1976, which was a poor year for the Chinese economy in most areas of production.[9]

Some sectors have fairly consistently reached the levels Chou En-lai described in 1975. These include cement, electric power generation, and crude oil production. The strategy of the new leadership group in Peking is to try to pull the lagging or frozen sectors such as steel—and railroad transport, which has also been in trouble for years—back up to at least the 10 percent a year range. It remains to be seen if this can be accomplished.*

---

*It should not be assumed that such growth is in contrast to absolute stagnation in China before the revolution of 1949. China was for hundreds of years one of the most advanced countries in the world, with a sizable skilled and literate urban population even in ancient times. John Gurley provides figures for China's industrial growth rate in the first decades of this century. For the period 1912 to 1936, that is, until the Japanese invasion, annual industrial output grew by 9.4 percent a year. This is approximately the same rate as the last decade and a half. (*China's Economy and the Maoist Strategy,* p. 104.)

Chiang Kai-shek showed no capacity to regain such growth rates at the end of World War II, when only a socialist revolution was able to put China on its feet. Nevertheless, these figures are striking, especially as they were sustained, until the outbreak of war, right through the Great Depression of the 1930s. (An important part of this output for the early 1930s was due to Japanese investment in Manchuria. But even excluding Manchuria altogether, Chinese industry expanded for the years 1931-36 at 6.7 percent a year.)

7. Agricultural Production and Population

China's success in feeding its large and growing population is no small accomplishment when millions in the semicolonial countries suffer from periodic famines or hover on the edge of starvation, and malnutrition shortens the lives of hundreds of millions more. On this score the abolition of capitalism and the institution of state direction of production and distribution has had the most dramatic and indisputable results. Compared to any country of Africa, Asia, or Latin America—with the exception of Cuba—China appears prosperous, judged by the food available to even its poorest citizens.

This victory remains a tenuous one, however, because it rests primarily on a relatively more rational and equitable distribution of foodstuffs and not yet on a decisive breakthrough in agricultural technology.

Many important problems for a strategy of development fall under the general heading of agriculture. The real growth of social wealth and in the standard of living of the masses is not a simple function of either industrial or agricultural growth, but a complex result of the combination of both. In a country such as China, where 80 percent of the population are peasants, agricultural production—that is, the ability of the society, above all, to feed its vast peasant masses and to provide a sufficient surplus to sustain its industrial sector—is a crucial indicator of the real standard of living.

China faces quite serious objective problems in the battle for the productivity of agricultural labor, rooted in its geography and history. The great contradiction of Chinese agriculture is that it has succeeded over thousands of years in greatly increasing the productivity of the land, but at the price of developing a method of agriculture that requires a very heavy investment of labor.

China's agricultural system is one of the marvels of early

agronomical science. It differs from European or American agriculture in that it is intensive, not extensive. That is, it resembles gardening more than it does farming in the West.

Relying on natural rainfall and the availability of large areas of uncultivated land, Western farmers before the advent of capitalism developed techniques that permitted small numbers of people, often single isolated families, to reap modest harvests from large tracts of land.

In China, agriculture has been tied from time immemorial to the need to mobilize large numbers of people to control the flow of rivers and to build irrigation works. The discovery of intensive methods of farming, such as the hand transplanting of rice seedlings, allowed a greater productivity of the land, and until recent historical times, of the individual worker as well. The social surplus product made possible by this type of agriculture was greater than in the West and sustained the relatively large urban population of China even in ancient times.

China is bordered by countries geographically hostile to the agricultural methods that formed the basis of its civilization. The grasslands of Mongolia, the desert and steppes of Chinese Turkestan, the mountainous highlands of Tibet, support only a sparse population, commonly nomadic herders, who in the past were a threat to the settled peoples of China. Hence the need for the Great Wall in the first place—both as a device to keep the nomads out and to keep the Chinese in so they would not mix in the affairs of others and draw attention to China.*

This meant that China developed historically in an area with definite geographical limits. Expansion could and did take place only southward. To the north and west lay barren lands; to the east the sea.

Although the land mass of China is large—slightly bigger than the United States—this fact is deceptive. Some 90 percent of China's territory is desert, mountains, tundra, or other surfaces unfit for cultivation. It is by nature poorly suited to be the most populous country. Its large population is really a measure of its success in wresting more from the land than other peoples had done.

If we compare China, the Soviet Union, and the United States on their relative arable land and population, this disparity is dramatically highlighted. The United States, with some 215

---

*See the classic work on this question, *Inner Asian Frontiers of China* by Owen Lattimore (New York: American Geographical Society, 1940).

million people, has roughly 1,200 million acres of arable land under cultivation. The Soviet Union, with 255 million people, has about 508 million acres. China, with 900 million people, has about 275 million acres. On a per capita basis, this means that in the U.S., 5.6 acres are cultivated per person; in the Soviet Union, two acres; but in China this figure is only one-third of an acre per person.[1]

Moreover, because China's intensive agricultural methods have been in use for centuries, there is little new land to be brought under cultivation. Most of the increases in agricultural output since 1949 have come from the use of fertilizers, high yield grains, water control, and mechanization.

With little arable land, the large tracts used in the U.S. for animal feed are not at present practical in China, severely limiting the amount of meat that can be added to the Chinese diet. In addition, labor-intensive Chinese garden farming is not so easily mechanized as the simple plowing operations of Western-style extensive agriculture.

Consequently, while once a world pace-setter in productivity, China remains so only in the yield per acre, and at the cost of very low productivity per person. The United States produces just slightly less grain than China in an average year. But it uses approximately 5 million people to do so, while China uses more than 700 million. Here is the crux of China's development problem.

In Chou En-lai's report to the Fourth National People's Congress in 1975, he offered two figures on agricultural productivity and one on population. He said that grain output had grown by an average of 4 percent a year "since liberation" (1949) and 4.2 percent a year in the decade 1964-74. And he added that population growth had been about 1.9 percent a year.[2]

If Chou's industrial figures did not tell the whole story, as we have already seen, his figures on agriculture come down to an outright misrepresentation. Again, the figures themselves do not lie, but they have been manipulated to imply something that is not true. The truth is that with the exception of two or three years, grain production has barely kept pace with population growth and in several periods has fallen seriously behind, leading to severe food shortages. China's improved distribution cushioned the impact of these setbacks, but at their worst, in the Great Leap disaster of the early 1960s, hunger was widespread. How is it possible for this to be true and Chou En-lai's statement to likewise be true? Chart 1 explains this apparent contradiction. As can be seen, Chou has taken as his base point two years of crisis in Chinese agriculture: the immediate end of the civil war and the mid-point of the Great Leap collapse. Not surprisingly, rapid growth follows for several years. But this is growth from the famine level back to an approximation of the consumption needs of China's people.

To be even more specific, Table 5 correlates the actual grain harvest for the twenty-four years between 1953 and 1976 with population growth. Dividing the harvest by the number of mouths to feed, the third column shows the pounds of grain per person per year for this whole period.

This table is one of the most significant indicators of the state of China's economy today and is worth examining closely. If the first two years and the last two are set aside, the intervening twenty show practically no improvement in the amount of food-grain per person available to China's people. Unquestionably there were important increases in total output—but these just kept pace with population growth.

And, while the statistics for the 1960-69 period are only approximations and do not have the evidential weight of the other years, they give some indication of the disaster of the Great Leap and the costs of the Cultural Revolution.

The figures tell us at the minimum that the amount of food available—particularly outside of the cities, which are considerably better off than the countryside—is not significantly greater today than it was in the 1950s. (Even with the apparently good ratio of food to population in 1976-77 there were reports from China of current food shortages.)

Beyond that we must proceed with caution. The crude correlation of total harvest to total population tells us only the outside limit of what individual food consumption might be. Obviously every person did not receive a straight 650 pounds of grain (rice, wheat, kaoliang, and millet) every year. On the production side, deductions from the total harvest must be made for industrial uses, including the production of alcoholic beverages, animal fodder, seed crop, and reserves. According to figures issued by Peking in the 1950s (no such breakdowns have been published since), these nonfood uses generally absorbed about 20 percent of the harvest. An additional 16 to 20 percent of the remaining figure is normally deducted for milling of rice to remove the hard outer casing. This last figure is quite variable, as in times of

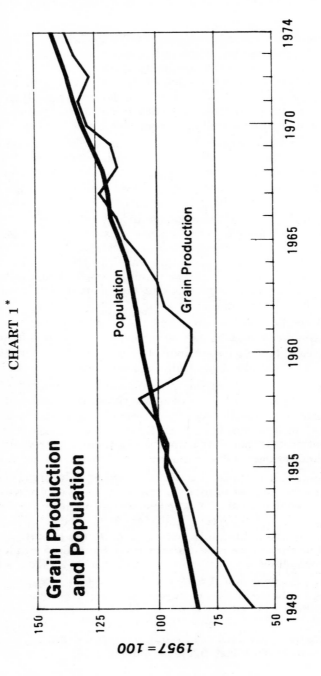

CHART 1*

Grain Production and Population

$1957 = 100$

*Source: John P. Hardt, "Summary," in Joint Economic Committee, U.S. Congress, *China: A Reassessment of the Economy* (Washington: U.S. Government Printing Office, 1975), p. 25.

TABLE 5
Production of Food Grains Correlated to Population Growth
1953-1976*

	Grain Harvest (mil. met. tons)	Population (millions)	Pounds of Grain Per Person Per Year
1953	157	583	593
1954	160	598	590
1955	175	606	637
1956	183	617	654
1957	185	629	649
1958	200**	641	688
1959	165**	653	557
1960	150	665	497
1961	162	678	527
1962	174	691	555
1963	183	704	573
1964	200	718	614
1965	205	731	618
1966	220	745	651
1967	230	759	668
1968	215**	774	613
1969	220**	788	616
1970	240	803	659
1971	246	819	662
1972	240	834	635
1973	250	850	649
1974	259	866	659
1975	280	883	699
1976	287***	900	703

*Sources: The harvest figures come from *China: A Reassessment of the Economy* (Washington: U.S. Government Printing Office, 1975), p. 351. In turn, the figures for 1955-57 are from the State Statistical Bureau pamphlet *Ten Great Years*; for 1970-73, from the Chinese press; and 1974 from Chou En-lai's January 1975 "Report on the Work of the Government." The series for 1960-67 have not been published by the Chinese, but were announced in meetings with foreign visitors and delegations. (**) The figures for 1958-59 and 1968-69, years respectively of the Great Leap and the Cultural Revolution, are from the *Far Eastern Economic Review*, October 3, 1975. The Joint Economic Committee considered information for these years too unreliable to offer a figure, so these should be regarded as estimates only. (***) The 1976 harvest total is from *FEER*, October 7, 1977.

On population, the 1953 figure of 583 million is from the 1953 census. The figure of 900 million for current population was issued in August 1977 (*New York Times*, November 5, 1977). For convenience, the figures in between are arrived at by multiplying the base year by the 1.9 percent a year growth rate announced by Chou En-lai in 1975. It comes out precisely at both ends of the time span. (For alternative estimates of population on a year by year basis, see Yuan-li Wu, *China: A Handbook* [New York: Praeger Publishers, 1973], pp. 868-83.)

The grain totals are for unhusked grain.

shortage less milling is done, in order to conserve the maximum possible food value.

On the other side of the equation, the population cannot be taken as an "average" whole. For example, children eat less than adults.

The Food and Agriculture Organization (FAO) of the United Nations compiled statistics on the actual yearly diet and consumption levels of the Chinese peasantry for twenty-two of China's provinces for the years 1931-37. These findings showed that 80 percent of all the calories in the peasants' diet came from grain, potatoes, and soybeans.[3]

John Lossing Buck, in *Land Utilization in China,* gave a somewhat higher figure: 89.6 percent.[4]

The FAO survey also showed that the actual grain available to the peasantry came to 512 pounds per person per year before milling. This was reduced after milling to about 411 pounds. This amounted to 1.13 pounds per person per day, most of it rice. The total calories in this grain were 1,771 per day. Supplemented by vegetables the daily intake by the peasantry was some 2,226 calories.

Was this prerevolutionary peasant diet adequate? International relief agencies operating in China at the end of World War II used the figure of 2,400 calories a day as adequate.[5]

This does not, on the other hand, make a slightly smaller 2,226 calorie a day diet equivalent to starvation. John Lossing Buck's studies offer a figure of what the absolute "minimum intake of energy value" is for China: 1,977 calories a day.[6] This, of course, is a bare subsistence diet, not the minimum required to be well fed.

Thus, the FAO's figures for the 1930s fall slightly above this absolute minimum level and slightly—or not so slightly—below the point at which hunger disappears, depending on what figures are used to establish this point.

Now let us turn to China in the 1950s. In 1957 the government published statistics for the average per capita consumption of the same basic foodstuffs surveyed in the 1930s: grains, potatoes, and soybeans. Its findings were as follows, for gross distribution before milling: 1953-54, 499 pounds; 1954-55, 515 pounds; and 1955-56, 538 pounds.[7]

Assuming the same number of calories per pound as in the 1930s, and roughly the same milling factor, this means that in 1953-54 the average per capita food consumption was below that in the 1930s; in 1954-55 it equaled it; and in 1955-56, surpassed it by a small margin.

At issue is not a question of allocating blame or of comparing the virtues as food growers of the Chinese workers' state and its capitalist predecessor. After 1937 China's economy foundered in the Japanese invasion and civil war, allowing population growth to gain a length on food production.

What is significant, however, is that per capita production in China peaked in 1955-56 and until 1975 had not advanced further.

The overall impression outsiders have of China is of relative food prosperity. That is not inconsistent with these figures. Most foreigners visit the cities and only a select number of agricultural communes in the countryside. Radical journalist K. S. Karol visited one commune where, in 1964, the total *yearly* income per person amounted to only a rice ration plus 50 yuan (US$26).[8]

It is possible, of course, that since the mid-1950s distribution has become better organized; that local disparities have been reduced; that a smaller percentage of agricultural produce is used in industry; or that other foodstuffs have supplemented rice and grain in the peasant diet. Still there are reasonable limits to all of these assumptions.

In 1957 Peking issued figures on meat consumption, broken down by city and countryside. At that time, the average amount of meat eaten in China was 15.4 pounds a year in the cities, slightly more than 1/2 ounce a day, and 8.5 pounds in the countryside.[9]

There are no official government statistics on the meat ration, issued later than 1960. There are, however, reports by Western visitors and journalists, such as this one from reporter Ross Munro:

Fresh meat is available only in limited quantities except just before holidays when supplies seem to be slightly more liberal. In some places there is a rigid rationing system; in other places the system is less formal with local shops selling only limited amounts to recognizable nearby residents. In Peking, where food seems to be more plentiful than anywhere else in China, the ration is one kilogram of meat per person per month. That works out to slightly more than an ounce each day. In many other areas, including Kunming in the southwest and Harbin in the northeast, the meat ration last winter was 8.8 ounces a month or, in other words, one quarter of the amount in Peking. In these areas, local officials tolerate extensive free markets in chickens and eggs so that people can supplement their meagre protein intake.[10]

There is, of course, room for error in such calculations. Their basic range, however, is not subject to serious doubt. Verification comes from several sources. First is the question of imports. China under imperialist domination had become a grain-importing country. One of the main aims of the First Five-Year Plan was agricultural self-sufficiency in order to free funds for industrial investment and, if possible, to finance industrial construction by the export of agricultural produce, as the Soviet Union had done in the 1930s and 1940s.

This goal was met briefly in the late 1950s. But since 1960 China has imported grain every single year, in the annual range of 3 million to 7 million tons.[11] This has been a serious drag on China's economy, as some 20 to 25 percent of all of its foreign purchases have gone for food.

A second indication of the actual state of affairs is the institution of rationing, beginning in 1953 and expanded in 1955. If there is not enough to eat, of course, it is better to ration what there is. But it should be remembered that there is no private business to speak of in China. The main purpose of such rationing of foodstuffs is not to prevent capitalist speculators from cornering the market. It is because, if they could get it, people would like to eat more. The rationing is in itself a sign that at least some people—and it would have to be a great many to justify such an elaborate and costly system as the ubiquitous ration tickets—do not get enough to eat. The *Far Eastern Economic Review*, for example, reported:

> Recent wallposters in Shanghai . . . have protested against the size of the rations of rice and cooking oil, and similar manifestations have been noted in Canton.[12]

One recent report comes from David Brown, a Canadian exchange student at Nanking University. He writes:

> Grain remains the staple food of the Chinese diet, students consuming 4 or 5 liang of rice each meal, or the equivalent in steamed bread. Although rationed, Chinese students receive a substantial 25 to 30 jin of grain [27.5-33 pounds] per month. More voracious students rely on the lesser appetites of their classmates, who sell their unused ration coupons.[13]

This ration is at most some 395 pounds per year, lower by 45 pounds than the official ration limit in 1957.[14] The point is not that Brown's classmates are not as well off as their predecessors twenty years ago. Many nongrain foodstuffs are in better supply now than then. What is significant here is that the ration level has decreased, not increased, in twenty years' time, and that it is set below the level of the normal range of consumption. To get enough food, students with big appetites engage in a little black-market trade in ration coupons.

(This is all quite good-natured among students. But there are wide income differentials in China. The majority of the peasantry, and the unskilled section of the urban working class, have very little cash income. Unlike David Brown's classmates, if their ration is insufficient they have no way to buy more. Moreover, the sale of state-assigned ration tickets, even if one had the money, is technically a serious crime, punishable by a long prison term. Plainly this law is not uniformly enforced. But equally plainly, choosing to deliberately break it is one thing for people the regime has nothing against, and a much more dangerous proposition for those under political suspicion, people who have antagonized local officials, or those branded as having "bad class background"—often not for their own deeds but for political affiliations or property ownership by their parents, grandparents, or even great-grandparents.)

None of this suggests that food has become significantly more abundant now than in the years of the First Five-Year Plan.

Finally, there is the case of the post–Great Leap period of agricultural decline. There is plenty of evidence that serious hunger and malnutrition were widespread in China in 1959-61. One typical account of the period was an interview in the July 25, 1959, Manchester *Guardian* with a woman refugee who had gone to Macao. She explained why she had left China:

First, because my husband had left the mainland last August; secondly, I couldn't stand to see my child starving. All the time he ate nothing but watery rice gruel, the only food available for the children. Look at him, he's 13 months old and he can't even crawl. . . . [There was] no meat, no vegetables, no nothing! Once in a while we eat rice with a kind of salty fluid which they say is used to preserve fish.

Since the mid-1960s, China has at least succeeded in warding off a repetition of this kind of calamity. But it has not changed the basic ratio of food to population, and that leaves the specter of hunger always standing by.

Ultimately these difficulties are surmountable, but what is required is the historical leap from vast agricultural backwardness to industrialization, including the industrialization of agriculture itself. Even within the framework of his commitment to the self-defeating theory of socialism in one country, Mao's particular policies for agriculture, promoted in the Great Leap Forward and in the Cultural Revolution, headed in a direction opposite to that of the objective needs of this process. He took the slogan of self-reliance, which is one-sided and isolationist even at the level of the nation-state, and sought to extend it to the level of the province, the county, and the peasant village. The government incessantly appealed for complete local self-sufficiency in foodstuffs and even in light industrial production of consumer goods and farm implements. While this had the advantage of reducing the demands on the state budget and of utilizing idle local resources, it moved away from an integrated national economy and planned industrial and agricultural growth. If the peasant must produce locally everything he or she consumes, the alliance with the urban industrial working class becomes inevitably endangered, as the cities come to appear to the peasant as an insatiable consumer of the peasants' grain while nothing comes back in the form of industrial products for use by the countryside.

It is a striking confirmation of the lack of actual working class control over the CCP leadership that such notions of rural self-isolation and self-sufficiency—ideas rooted in China's precapitalist past—could have been seriously promulgated by the government. Much of this rhetoric has been abandoned now that Mao is gone, but the new government hasn't formulated any alternative line.

Until China can free a majority of those who now labor on the land for other work it will not be able to close the gap that separates it from the standard of living that has already been achieved for working people in the advanced capitalist countries. There are some romantics or admirers of Maoism who would argue that such an aspiration is mere useless consumerism. Such a view runs counter to all of Marxist thought, not to speak of the rightful demands of the masses. Working people cannot truly participate equally in political life while they are prohibited from moving from one place to another, or while the sheer struggle for existence requires that they labor "from dawn to dusk almost every day of the year," as the doctor from Shanghai put it to Joshua Horn. That kind of grinding necessity must be overcome by the increase in social wealth and culture before we can speak seriously of socialist freedom.

8. The Overall Growth of Social Wealth

We have seen some of the achievements made possible by the abolition of capitalist private property in China. We have also seen the great distance that China must cover to overtake and surpass the standard of living of the industrially advanced countries. This is a burning problem that confronts not only the people of China but the majority of the human race, who live today under conditions comparable to those China faced in 1949. In later chapters we will come to other measures of the quality of human life that socialism should and must provide—democratic rights, the genuine submission of governmental representatives to control by the working masses, material and political equality. But here we must examine a central rationalization of bureaucratic rule: that the handing over of absolute power to the party and state bureaucracy guarantees, at the minimum, a far more rapid increase in the standard of living than capitalism can ensure.

This claim, repeated on every occasion by the bureaucrats and their apologists, is true, but only partially and in a highly conditional way. A planned economy is capable of real economic "miracles," but not if it is crippled by the exclusion of the masses from formulating the plan, and not while it is locked into the straitjacket of national communism. This may appear to some as a mere assertion of doctrinaire Marxism. There is a way to test its validity. That is, to compare China's overall rate of growth to that of the capitalist semicolonies. Obviously some countries in the colonial world began this century from a more developed industrial base than China, so what is at issue is not the absolute standard of living of their peoples or the magnitude of their industrial output, but the pace of their development.

Many writers, ranging from academic liberals to the contributors to *Monthly Review,* accept as though it is a proven fact that China's growth rate is considerably greater than any of the

75

capitalist semicolonies—with the exception of such artificial hothouse projects of American imperialism as Taiwan and South Korea, or the oil-producing countries of the Middle East. How true is this assumption?

If China's industrial growth is 10 percent a year or less, and agricultural growth is about 2 percent, annual growth of Gross National Product (GNP) must be somewhere in the middle. If population growth is taken into account, per capita growth in GNP will be lower still. Several Western economists have made computations of these results on the basis of the few figures released by the Chinese government. A U.S. government economist made a computation of the overall growth of the Chinese economy for the years 1958-74. He came up with the following (annual percentages of growth): GNP, 5.2; agricultural production, 2.0; industrial output, 9.0; population, 2.1; and per capita GNP, 3.0.[1]

Comparable figures are given by Carl Riskin, an American China scholar and economist sympathetic to the Chinese revolution:

. . . China's GDP [Gross Domestic Product] for the entire two decades after 1952 grew at an average rate of 4.6 to 6 per cent, depending on the prices and industrial output indexes used. Subtracting roughly two per cent to take account of China's population growth rate over this period (probably an overgenerous allowance) produces a range of 2.6 to 4 per cent for the average growth of GDP per capita for the two decades.[2]

So, then, roughly 5.5 percent a year overall growth in gross domestic output and 3 percent per capita has been China's actual performance for the last twenty years and more. How have comparable countries fared that are still subject to foreign exploitation? Carl Riskin gives the following figures:

Thus, the 42 poorest countries categorised as "least developed" by the UN classification system, experienced an average annual growth rate in *aggregate* GNP of only 1.1 per cent for the period 1965 to 1974, while the remaining 55 "developing" nations grew by an average of 3.3 per cent per year over the same period. The average *per capita* income growth rates implied by these figures are substantially inferior to China's recent record. Of Asian LDCs [Least Developed Countries], a number had significantly higher growth rates than China, but none in China's income class except Indonesia (an OPEC member) did as well.[3]

Figures on GNP are difficult to correlate. Riskin's are based on a study by economist Michael Todaro, *Economic Development in the Third World,* published in London in 1977. The United Nations offers a different set of figures which suggest that if Riskin's figures for the 42 poorest countries are correct, his figures for the slightly better off semicolonies are too low.

Table 6 provides the UN statistics for the period 1963-73. The UN's figures are for "developing countries," which here include both the poorest and the next level, but do not include either the imperialist countries or the workers' states. The breakdown is by region. West Asia includes oil-producing countries of the Middle East and therefore should not be counted as typical.

These figures, for Africa, East Asia, and Latin America, would place China, at some 5.5 percent a year growth in GNP and 3 percent per capita, at no better than the average for these regions.

Now, let us try one last approximation. We have seen from Riskin's figures that China has done considerably better than the very poorest countries of the world. And the UN statistics suggest that it has not done any better than the average. What is needed is a comparison of some selected countries, since heavy imperialist investment in a few countries distorts averages for a region, as does oil in Venezuela or Indonesia, as well as in the Middle East.

The *Far Eastern Economic Review* in its *Asia 1977 Yearbook* gives its estimates of the average annual growth of GNP for Asia for the period 1960-73. Its findings are given in Table 7.

China, then, is doing better than the most miserable of the colonial slaves of world imperialism. It is striking, however, how slim China's lead is over the next group of semicolonies. If there is any lead at all. Often relatively small amounts of imperialist investment serve to boost the growth rates of the semicolonies ahead of China's. If this were limited to Taiwan and South Korea it could be dismissed as unrepeatable. But scores of countries, from Brazil to Malaysia and Thailand, are actually growing as fast as China. Of course, their distribution systems are more unfair than China's. But surely socialism (even in a bureaucratic stranglehold) should be able to outproduce these client regimes and not actually fall behind them.

It is still more striking that a country such as Indonesia, with its brutal military dictatorship, could be growing faster than China, even given its oil income. Indonesia has a big population—129 million—and therefore its statistics are not so easily distorted by a particular raw material export as would be the case, say, in the Arab oil-exporting nations. China also is an oil-producing country. Indonesia's rate of growth of Gross Domestic Product (GDP), though low in the early 1960s, for the years

TABLE 6

United Nations Estimate of Annual Average Growth
Rate of Semicolonial World, 1963-73, by Region*

Region	Gross Domestic Product	Per Capita
Africa	5.1	2.4
East Asia and Pacific**	5.4	2.7
West Asia (inc. Mid. East)	8.5	5.1
Latin America and Caribbean	5.5	2.7

*United National Economic and Social Council, Commission for Social Development, *1974 Report on the World Social Situation: Social Trends: A Global Overview* (November 12, 1974), p. 10. (**)Does not include China.

TABLE 7

Annual Average % Growth of Gross National Product
for Selected Asian Countries, 1960-73*

Country	% Average GNP Growth
Afghanistan	2.5
Bangladesh	2.4
China	5.5
India	3.6
Indonesia	4.4
Japan	10.5
Laos	3.0
Malaysia	6.5
Pakistan	4.5
Philippines	5.3
Sri Lanka	4.3
Taiwan	9.9
Thailand	7.9

Asia Yearbook 1977 (Hong Kong: Far Eastern Economic Review, 1977), p. 14.

1969-73 was 8.7 percent per year, almost twice that of China, and its per capita growth of GDP for the same period was 4.9 percent, again higher than China's.[4]

One common comparison is between China and India, because of the gigantic size of both populations and their impoverished starting point. We have noted the stagnation and sluggish growth of important sectors of Chinese industry. India has done much worse. By 1973 China's steel output was 4.3 times that of India; coal, 4.6 times; crude oil, 7.2; chemical fertilizer, 3.5; and sewing machines, 13 times.[5]

Still, as commanding as China's lead is, it took twenty-five years of development in national isolation to achieve it, and it is to this day marked by important weak spots. China has 1.6 times the population of India. This means that it must produce 1.6 times as much of a commodity to match India's output on a per capita basis. As late as 1969, China's per capita production was lower than India's in cotton cloth, sugar, bicycles (the main means of transport for ordinary people), radios, cement, electric power, and motor vehicles. It was barely ahead in foodgrains. Even by 1973, China had no significant edge in food production, bicycles, or electric power.[6]

The most dramatic difference between China and India is not in gross industrial output. It is in social responsibility. In India today, some 300 million people, almost half the population, live below not just the poverty line but the destitution line—actually in hunger. In China such misery has been eliminated.

One measure of social wealth that we have not touched on is the actual standard of living of the urban working class. It does not follow that a 3 percent per year increase in per capita income means that this is really distributed to individuals. What has been the situation in this pivotal sector? The Mao regime chose to retain this increment and use it for further investment and for the consumption of the bureaucracy.

John Gurley tells us frankly: "Since 1957-1958 . . . wage policy has swung toward direct controls over labor allocation and toward attempts to keep urban wages from rising very much. . . ."[7]

Gurley estimates that, after an initial spurt between 1949 and 1952, real wages of Chinese workers rose by an annual average of only 1.9 percent between 1952 and 1972. But even at that, virtually all of that increase had already been given by 1957, and the next raise did not come until twenty years later, after Mao's death!

It was only in October 1977 that the new regime finally made a real concession on this long-standing grievance of the Chinese working class. Yu Ch'iu-li in his economic report to the Standing Committee of the Fourth National People's Congress announced the first across-the-board wage raise in two decades. He did not indicate the actual amounts, but he did say it would begin at once and would affect "about forty-six per cent of the total number of workers and staff."[8]

Yu's report, cited earlier, indicated in various ways the setbacks to China's economic development under the Mao government. Some other recent accounts should be considered that describe the effects of this on the working class.

One striking report came from two Canadian Maoists, Pat and Roger Howard, who work for the Chinese government in Canton. The Howards are now supporters of Hua Kuo-feng. They wrote three articles for the American weekly *Guardian* in March 1977 to rebuff some of the *Guardian*'s criticisms of Hua. In explaining why they considered the purge of the "gang of four" necessary, the Howards described the economic deterioration they had witnessed during the time they lived in Canton:

There have been serious problems with production in a number of areas since the cultural revolution and the situation has worsened in some areas in recent years. . . . In Canton, the supply of basic food items has deteriorated noticeably in the last few years because of disruption of agricultural planning and the supply system. In Wenchow in Chekiang province, where a "rebel" named Weng Sen-he with the support of Wang Hung-wen led factional struggles which literally destroyed the collective economy, shortages led to the growth of speculation, black markets, the growth of private enterprises and even division of the land to attempt individual production.[9]

And further:

. . . many ordinary people in China were finding it more and more difficult to buy food and other daily necessities because of the disruptions in production and distribution due to interference by the four in planning and production.

None of this, of course, appeared in the carefully controlled press. . . .[10]

In February 1977 the shortages were still widespread and were beginning to be reported in the regular Chinese press. The *Far Eastern Economic Review* later wrote:

At the Chinese New Year, serious food shortages were reported even from Canton, reflecting the chaos which had afflicted many sectors of the economy over the past few months. The *People's Daily* said in February that it would take between three and five years to restore the disorder on the railways.[11]

This gives some insight into the problems of day-to-day life for ordinary people in China. There is another end to the spectrum; the opulent life of the powerful bureaucracy. For them, the promise of plenty under socialism is not a distant hope. It has already arrived.

Part III
The Society

9. The Privileged Caste

The soldiers in the guerrilla armies of Mao and Chu Te were ragged and hungry when they took power in 1949. A close look at the commanding strata headquartered in Yenan before taking power would show, however, that they were not quite so poor. This leadership, after all, headed a government that ruled tens of millions of people for more than a decade before it came to national power. Privileges are relative, and in the midst of civil war the luxuries that later became available in Peking were unthinkable. This historical origin of the Maoist leadership left its stamp. It takes the form of a moral injunction to consume inconspicuously.

In the capitalist West, the old money of the dominant ruling families looks on extravagant displays of spending by the nouveau riche as in bad taste. The Soviet bureaucracy became notorious for just this kind of crude, arrogant luxury living. The Chinese Stalinists, in contrast, adhere to the view that the less obvious their privileges are, the less opposition they will encounter. The Cultural Revolution, in particular, was waged under slogans of eliminating inequality, abolishing ranks, reviving "plain living," etc. A good description of what actually happened is provided by Simon Leys, a keenly observant Belgian art historian and Sinologist, in an account of a six-month visit in 1972. He writes:

In trains . . . first, second, and third classes have disappeared *in name,* but you have now "sitting hard" (*ying tso*), "sleeping hard" (*ying wo*), and "sleeping soft" (*juan wo*), which are exactly the same classes as before and with the fares, as before, ranging from single to triple prices. External insignia have nearly completely disappeared in the army; they have been replaced by a loose jacket with four pockets for officers, two pockets for privates. In this way, a colonel traveling first-class on the railway is now merely a four-pocket military man "sleeping soft"—with a two-pocket man respectfully carrying his suitcase. In cities one can still distinguish between four-pocket men in jeeps, four-pocket men in black limousines with curtains, and four-pocket men who have black limousines with curtains and a jeep in front.[1]

The CCP has never made a secret of the wage differentials in the salary structure it has imposed on China since 1949. Generally its propagandists try to explain this away by pointing to inevitable inequalities under a transitional economy emerging directly from capitalism in a poor country. The point is true enough in the abstract. But it is the scale that transforms the argument from truth to sophistry. Lenin and the Bolsheviks adopted a wage scale that paid government and party functionaries in the Soviet Union no more than the pay of a skilled worker. Salary differentials in the early Bolshevik government were no more than five to one, and the higher ranges were paid to specialists and technicians, not the party cadres.[2]

In 1956, the Chinese government adopted a system of ranks for state employees that included thirty grades, with the top grade receiving no less than twenty-eight times the pay of the bottom grade![3] In addition to salaries, higher cadres and state officials have expense accounts that provide special housing, cars, drivers, staffs (including private servants), meals, travel, etc.

Using devices such as the four-pocket military tunic, the CCP hierarchy hides much of its most extravagant living from the prying eyes of ordinary citizens and foreigners. We are indebted to the few reports of those who have entered this charmed circle for what we know about the standard of living of China's rulers. One of the best-known accounts of the 1950s was that of Chow Ching-wen in his book *Ten Years of Storm*.

Chow Ching-wen was a former president of Northeastern University in Manchuria and a leader of the liberal bourgeois China Democratic League. He participated in the coalition government set up by the CCP in 1949, and was a top government functionary in Peking until 1957, when he fled to Hong Kong. By the time he wrote his book, Chow had become a bitter opponent of the Maoist regime. That must be taken into account in weighing his testimony. But he was certainly in a position to see what he described. Let us quote Chow's report, then see whether it can be substantiated from other sources:

The heads of departments and people of ministerial rank have special coupons for meat, game, fowl, and other delicacies and are not restricted to rations. Every morning, long lines of jeeps and trucks are at the market to bring back food for the VIP's, and it is only after their needs have been satisfied that the people are allowed to buy what they can. Furthermore, every VIP has a chef of some renown to cook for him. This is perhaps one of the "achievements" the CC are most proud of. Every time I had a meal with a VIP, he boasted about his chef, who was formerly either the chef of some famous restaurant or distinguished household. Once, at the home of one of the VIP's, I even tasted food prepared by the former chef of Henry Pu Yi, the last Emperor of the Ching Dynasty.[4]

When the VIPs of the CCP want to get away from the city (for them life should not be all work and no play), they go to the sumptuous villas which the capitalists, foreigners, and reactionary politicians had built at the resorts. . . .

By special trains they arrive—the higher echelon of the Communist Government, with large families and an entourage of cooks, nurses, and doctors in tow. But as I have said, even with the members of the new aristocracy, there are differences in the extent of special privileges enjoyed. The highest of the high may have whatever their hearts desire so long as it is for sale, in China or in any country in the world. The scale of privileges comes down according to the positions the members occupy in the regime. But as long as one has power over someone else—whether it extends to the entire country or merely to the limits of a village or county—despotic rights come with it, and in material comfort one is sure to be better off than those over whom one has power. The high in office draw openly from the National Treasury for their expenses. The smaller despots get what they want direct from the people.[5]

If anyone is disposed to believe that Chow invents this, or even exaggerates, out of political malice, there are today's revelations by the Chinese government itself about the corruption of its highest leaders under Mao Tsetung. Some of these reports on the spending sprees of Wang Hung-wen and the imperial conduct of Chiang Ch'ing have already been cited. One of the greatest breaches in the curtain of secrecy with which the Chinese leadership surrounds itself is Chiang Ch'ing's own memoirs, dictated to American scholar Roxane Witke in 1972.

In a certain sense, Peking's present charge that Chiang Ch'ing's interviews with Witke revealed state secrets is true because she opened a peephole into the private life of China's rulers, which has indeed been a closely guarded and highly damaging secret.

Let us follow Roxane Witke on her initiation into the imperial court. Actually nothing much has changed since the revels of the 1950s described by Chow Ching-wen, except that today the VIPs get to their out-of-town villas by plane instead of train. In this case, one August evening in 1972, Chiang Ch'ing had preceded her guest to her secluded mansion in Canton, then sent her private plane back to Shanghai to pick up Witke and several interpreters.

Yü, Lao Ch'en, and I were ushered onto a field deserted by all but one great silver jet. . . .

The aircraft's spacious and well-designed interior was far from the Chinese ordinary. Chang Ying and I were directed to the forward cabin, which was equipped with writing and dining tables, electronic fittings, and a full-sized bed covered with delicately embroidered silk sheets and a matching pillow of pale pink and white. . . . two spectacularly pretty PLA girls delivered plates of roast duck, various sweet-meats, freshly steamed buns, exquisite fruits, ice cream, liquors, beer and wines.[6]

Witke describes Chiang Ch'ing's retreat:

Leading to Chiang Ch'ing's villa was a narrow winding road flanked by deep bamboo groves. In them young PLA guards, bayonets glinting, were partially hidden. The villa, a rangy single-story modern building, stood in quiet reserve, surrounded by tropical gardens: climbing bougainvillea, hibiscus in hot colors, pink-tinged lotus blossoms floating on reflecting pools, redolent magnolia, jasmine, and ginger blossoms, the pulsating screams of cicadas, and the atonal descant of birds.[7]

And so it goes. Chiang Ch'ing "was wearing a superbly tailored shirtwaist dress of heavy crepe de chine, with a full pleated skirt falling to midcalf."[8] Further samples:

Each evening Chiang Ch'ing drew her narrative to a close only on the repeated insistence of her bodyguards and nurses and on intermittent signals from her two personal physicians, who paced the floor or observed her quietly from remote sections of the room.[9]

The second evening we moved to a larger villa (though Chiang Ch'ing continued to live in the first), one with more rooms that could be used in succession as the sultry southern air grew stale.[10]

One evening after a late dinner in Canton and a gracious promenade around a hall in her villa, Chiang Ch'ing revealed that she had a treat in store: Garbo's *Queen Christina*. Her face was glowing with anticipation. That Metro-Goldwyn-Mayer film of 1933 was an old favorite of hers. She had ordered it flown down from Peking for the evening's entertainment. Her personal archive of foreign and Chinese films included a nearly complete collection of Garbo.[11]

To give an idea of what our meals were like, dinner the first night at the villa in Canton opened with roasted cashew nuts, tomato and cucumber salad, and thinly sliced smoked ham. Then came three-yellow chicken served with ginger sauce—a Cantonese specialty—and tiny birds, possibly thrushes, which were deep-fried and consumed whole, crackling to the teeth. Two dishes of crab meat, one sweet water and the other saltwater, were turned out in different styles. The chicken congee, which is rice cooked in a rich chicken broth, had edible white jasmine blossoms floating on the surface. Mushrooms and other fresh vegetables were pantossed and served without sauce. . . .

Chiang Ch'ing's cooks were versatile—masters of regional Chinese dishes and also skilled in foreign cooking. One most memorable meal was "Western," but presented in the Chinese style. There were the usual ten courses, but each was a meal in itself: a succession of steak and fried potatoes, fried chicken and mashed potatoes, a "curry" and rice, fried fish, a series of overboiled vegetables, and deliberately composed salads. The desert I have forgotten.[12]

Everything Chow Ching-wen observed about the opulence of the upstart Maoist bureaucracy of the 1950s has since become ingrained habit and the expected perquisites of power at the top. The entourage of servants, private cooks, special supplies of expensive, exotic, and finely prepared foods, private mansions. Chiang Ch'ing's official salary was 400 yuan a month—some US$208. That is a munificent sum in China—a year's pay for an unskilled worker or a peasant. But no one could suggest that the scale of regal luxury indulged in by Chiang Ch'ing could have been paid for by $208 a month, even at China's low prices. And in 1972, even by the government's present accounts, she was still living with Mao.

One final piece of testimony from Roxane Witke. Chiang Ch'ing not only had unlimited money, the right to command huge staffs of servants, but also the power to use "her" soldiers to rope off public parks and gardens for days at a time for the private enjoyment of herself and her friends. Witke writes:

Although she did not have *Dream of the Red Chamber*'s famous garden, Ta-kuan-yuan, at her disposal, for the duration of her Canton retreat she had reserved for her pleasure something comparable: an orchid park stretching between her villa and the Pearl River. . . .

We arrived separately at Chiang Ch'ing's lush secret garden. Chang Ying led my guides and me along winding paths, pointing out the most exotic of the hundreds of varieties of orchids along the way. At a gentle pace we passed through moongates, traversed gardens skillfully land-scaped "naturalistically," bypassed rustic tea pavilions, and crossed arched bridges over artificial streams and ponds. . . . In the hazy distance arose a moonviewing pavilion. Chiang Ch'ing, dressed in luminous silk, was seated on its veranda overlooking a lotus pond.[13]

Only an emperor and empress can live quite on that scale. Lower down in the pecking order the elite bureaucrats come into more frequent contact with the masses and are seen more often. John Burns, for example, writing from Peking, describes his observations of the life of middle-ranking cadres:

Of course, senior cadres have expenses that workers do not. Typically, they will have an apartment of several rooms, perhaps even a house, for which they will pay as much as 50 yuan ($28) a month, compared to the dollar or two paid by workers for their 2½ rooms.

A tailor-made worsted tunic at 150 yuan ($85) against a worker's 25 yuan ($14) denims, is part of every cadre's wardrobe, and leather shoes, also de rigeur, run up to 40 yuan ($22) a pair, 10 times what a worker pays for his plastic or canvas knockarounds.

All this, however, leaves a surplus. A cadre can put this on deposit at the bank, for a nominal interest rate of less than 1 per cent, and many do. Deposits of as much as 5,000 yuan ($2,860) are not unknown. He can also indulge in a few luxuries: a Rolex watch at 918 yuan ($515) is the ultimate in cachet (a department store in Nanking, a city of less than two million, sold more than 100 of the next-best Omega model, at 650 yuan ($365) last year) and black-and-white television sets at 450 yuan ($260) are becoming increasingly popular (the same Nanking store sold more than 500 to individuals in 1974).[14]

Insofar as the faction now in power has any discernible differences from the Mao group on the question of privilege it is that Teng and his supporters have always taken their graft as a matter of course, with fewer hypocritical campaigns against "bourgeois rights." Chiang Ch'ing was the specialist in inveighing against high-living officials.

10. Peking's Foreign Policy

Many young radicals around the world were drawn to Maoism after the open rift between Peking and Moscow in 1960. China stood sharply to the left of the Soviet government, at least in words, on many important issues of world politics, above all on the need for an uncompromising struggle against imperialist domination of the semicolonial nations.

Maoism's appeal was strengthened by China's support to the people of Vietnam after the massive American invasion of Vietnam in 1965. The obvious justice of Vietnam's cause was often taken as the starting point of a broader generalization: that Maoism or the "Third World" or some similar entity embodied the aspirations for emancipation of the millions oppressed by capitalism and colonialism.

In recent years there has been considerable consternation among Western Maoists and quasi-Maoists over what they have taken to be serious mistakes in China's foreign policy. These range from Peking's courtship of Richard Nixon to its support for NATO or its refusal to call for support to the fight of the Angolan MPLA against the South African intervention in Angola in 1975-76 and its backing of the repressive Mobutu regime in Zaïre.

The most elementary axiom of Marxism on this question is that the international policy of states is inseparable from and subordinate to their internal social structure and national needs. Foreign policy is an extension of the domestic policy of the decision-makers in power. Peking's détente with American imperialism is not a "mistake," but a calculated strategy to meet the inner needs of its Stalinist bureaucracy.

This fact may be obscured by the leftist and even ultraleftist posturing of Peking during the early years of the Sino-Soviet dispute and the Vietnam War. Most people in the West who became sympathetic to Maoism did so on the basis of the radical things Peking said in the mid-1960s. What is necessary here is to distinguish its radical rhetoric from the actual course of Peking's foreign policy. After the Soviet government callously withdrew its aid and technicians from China in 1960 and left the people of China to fend for themselves, Peking said some correct things about the reactionary nature of the Moscow regime, and also about the nature of world imperialism, which was then looking for an opening to intervene against the Chinese revolution. Similarly in the Vietnam War, which ultimately threatened not only Hanoi, but Peking itself. Mao and the rest of the CCP leadership offered aid—albeit very limited—to the side of the Vietnamese fighters against the American aggression.*

But these were conjunctural reactions to immediate threats. The fundamental orientation of Stalinism, flowing from its very social nature, is to seek the preservation of the status quo and accommodation with existing capitalist governments. Its nationalism makes it disinterested in, and even opposed to, the spread of socialist revolution beyond the borders it controls. Its privileges and fear of the working class and peasantry at home lead it to sense an affinity with governments based on minority rule in other parts of the world.

The record of the CCP in power, both domestic and foreign, may seem to clash with its previous history, the twenty years and more of guerrilla struggle in the Chinese countryside. The heroism of the Long March inspired a generation of fighters in China and around the world and appeared to hold out the promise of something better than the ossified theocracy constructed by the CCP after 1949. The disparity is rooted not in the thoughts of Mao Tsetung but in the social forces he represented.

After the debacle of the revolution of 1925-27, brought about by the subordination of the young Chinese Communist Party to the Kuomintang of Chiang Kai-shek, the CCP went through a strategic reorientation. Mao Tsetung was instrumental in this, although until 1935 he remained in a minority in the party. The Chinese Communists turned away from the cities; not only from the centers of capitalist power that had decimated their ranks, but also from the working class, which had given the party its social cohesion as a force for socialism.

---

*In point of fact, the Soviet Union actually supplied more aid to the Vietnamese resistance than China did. According to the best available estimates, between 1966 and 1972 the USSR sent $2.4 billion to Vietnam compared to $1.7 billion from China. In the same period Washington spent $101 billion to prop up the counterrevolutionary Saigon regime. (U.S. Department of Defense figures, cited by *New Times,* August 9, 1974.)

The party flourished, fed by the wellsprings of peasant discontent and its militant methods of struggle. But its social outlook, composition, and ultimate aims were molded by its new environment. This process was speeded by the purges of proletarian revolutionists, by the Stalinist ideology of the leading cadres, and by pressure from the Soviet government, which was concerned not with socialist revolution in China but with securing a friendly government on its frontier.

In place of a party of workers in alliance with and leading a peasant movement of revolt, the CCP became a party of peasants, led by displaced city intellectuals acting in the name of a working class that was present in name only. Mao and his generals proved themselves capable mass leaders and military commanders in the unfolding peasant revolution. Yet the ultimate aims of the struggle became more and more amorphous. After the 1937 compact with the KMT against the Japanese invasion, socialism became a distant and unreal goal; the party's announced objective was a postwar coalition government with Chiang Kai-shek, a democratized China that would permit the dissolution of the CCP's armies and its integration into a modernized and forward-looking capitalist state. Despite the military means used by Mao to promote this aim, its content was reformist rather than revolutionary. An example is Mao's attitude toward the American government and toward Chiang Kai-shek near the end of World War II, that is, after the threat from Japanese imperialism, which had been the original justification of the bloc with Chiang, had receded. Mao at that time welcomed the intervention of U.S. imperialism into Chinese politics through the person of General Patrick Hurley, and he applauded Franklin Roosevelt's efforts to reconcile the CCP and Chiang Kai-shek's Kuomintang, himself proposing the formation of a coalition government. In a letter to Roosevelt dated November 10, 1944, Mao wrote:

My Dear President Roosevelt: I am greatly honored in receiving your personal representative, General Patrick Hurley. During his three day visit here in Yenan we have congenially discussed all the problems concerning the unity of all Chinese people and all the military forces for the defeat of Japan and reconstruction of China. For this I have offered an agreement.
. . . It has always been our desire to reach an agreement with President Chiang Kai-shek which will promote the welfare of the Chinese people. Through the good offices of General Hurley we have suddenly seen hope of realization. It is with great pleasure that I express my high appreciation for the excellent talent of your Personal Representative and his deep sympathy towards the Chinese people.

The Central Committee of our Party has unanimously accepted the whole text of this proposed agreement and is prepared to fully support and to make it effective. . . .
. . . I wish also to thank you, Mr. President, for your great labors in the interests of the unity of China for the defeat of Japan and for making possible a united, democratic China.[1]

The operative clause in the agreement that Mao speaks of here reads: "The present National Government is to be reorganized into a Coalition National Government embracing representatives of all anti-Japanese parties and non-partisan political bodies."[2]

The final break with Chiang came at Chiang's initiative, not Mao's, when the KMT rejected the CCP's demand for one-third representation for itself and its allies in China's postwar Political Consultative Conference and launched a military offensive against the CCP in July 1946. Even then, the CCP hesitated until October 1947 to accede to peasant demands for land reform in the territories it controlled—the final symbolic act that made reconciliation with Chiang impossible.

The CCP in the years between 1927 and 1949 remained a workers' party only in a restricted sense of that term as it is usually understood. Blows directed against it by domestic and foreign capitalism were aimed at the working class as well as at the party itself. Its ties with world Stalinism and its claim to speak for the workers of China made it a participant in the world workers' movement. Its victory over Chiang Kai-shek greatly strengthened its influence among socialists in every country. But military victory, and even the abolition of capitalist property which followed in 1952-53 under the impact of capitalist sabotage during the Korean War, did not of themselves vindicate the CCP's claim to embody the class interests of China's workers. Other social strata have in the past—and since—stood between the old rulers and the oppressed, led movements of revolt, and even taken state power. Not the least of these precedents come from China's own history, marked as it is by a succession of peasant revolutions—the last of these, the T'aip'ing rebellion, seized half of China between 1851 and 1864 and was defeated only with the aid of foreign imperialism, despite the fact that its leaders were authoritarian Christian mystics with no clear idea of what they would do with the power if they won.

The ultimate test of the actual nature of the CCP lies not in the struggle that led to power but in the character of the regime created afterward. Part of the measure of that regime is its attitude toward world capitalism. This can be gauged from the high points of Chinese diplomacy since the founding of the People's Republic, from the Geneva conference of 1954 to Nixon's visit to Peking.

The Geneva conference convened in May 1954 to decide the fate of formerly French Indochina after the Viet Minh had dealt its stunning military defeat to the French at Dienbienphu. The whole of Vietnam was in the hands of the liberation forces, and French colonialism was in no position to continue the war. Yet at Geneva the imperialists were able to win at the bargaining table something they were incapable of taking on the battleground. This occurred in a sudden and unexpected concession by the delegations from the Viet Minh, Russia, and China, after five weeks of deadlock. The concession was to agree to withdraw Vietnamese forces to the seventeenth parallel and permit the reestablishment of a French puppet government in the South. This provided the foothold imperialism required to relaunch its war of aggression against the Vietnamese people a few years later.

Given the terrible price that the people of Vietnam later paid for this generosity to their enemies, how did they agree to such a proposal in 1954 in the first place? The Pentagon Papers, published in 1971, for the first time gave the U.S. government's inside account of what transpired at Geneva. The Defense Department analysts wrote:

While it is fair to state that the immediate implications of the Accords did not reflect (even according to CIA reports) Viet Minh strength and control in Vietnam at the time of the conference, it is equally important to understand why. Viet Minh ambitions were thwarted, not so much by Western resistance or treachery, as by Sino-Soviet pressures on them to cooperate. . . . Together and separately, Moscow and Peking pressed concessions on the Viet Minh. Invariably, the two principal communist delegates, Chou En-lai and Molotov, played major roles in breaking deadlocks with conciliatory initiatives. . . . "Peaceful co-existence" was the hallmark of their diplomacy. The Chinese, in particular, were interested in border security, buffers, preventing the formation of a U.S. alliance system with bases in the region, and reconstruction at home. The two big communist powers did not hesitate in asserting the paramountcy of their interests over those of the Viet Minh.[3]

That same year, Peking announced that the basis of its foreign policy was the "Five Principles of Peaceful Coexistence." During the early years of the Sino-Soviet split, Peking no longer mentioned this, and even went so far as to say—correctly—that peaceful coexistence with imperialism is equivalent to class collaboration and is a betrayal of the interests of the working class. But even in those years the olive branch was always extended to any capitalist government willing to do business with China. Since 1971 the "Five Principles" have been revived and once more are acknowledged as the guideline of China's foreign relations.

These "principles" are enumerated as (1) mutual respect for territorial integrity and sovereignty, (2) nonaggression, (3) noninterference in each other's internal affairs, (4) equality and mutual benefit, and (5) peaceful coexistence.

Since when have Marxists pledged themselves not to interfere in struggles between working people and their rulers because these are the "internal affairs" of the capitalist nation-state? It is worth recalling that this list was not drafted unilaterally by China but was first published in a joint communiqué signed by Chou En-lai and Nehru in New Delhi in June 1954. Afterwards they were written into the 1954 constitution of the People's Republic of China. It is understandable that Nehru was pleased to accept China's promise not to interfere in Indian politics on the side of the Indian masses. But what are we to think of the socialist or communist pretensions of a regime that would make such a pledge?

Perhaps this was all tongue-in-cheek, the usual rigamarole of diplomacy, which should not be taken seriously. There are defenders of Maoism who advance this claim. It is necessary, this line of reasoning goes, to lie to the class enemy, to put him off his guard, and thereby make the ultimate victory easier. If this were truly Peking's intent it would be at best misguided—an attempt to employ the methods of bourgeois duplicity to manipulate a revolution into existence behind the backs of the masses. After all, who is more easily fooled by such stratagems—the wily and experienced leaders of world capitalism, or the masses just emerging into political consciousness? How are the workers of India supposed to know that the Chinese Communist Party is only feigning its friendship for their rulers, while the capitalist class of India is to be kept in the dark and not let in on this little joke at their expense?

Unfortunately, the record of Peking's diplomacy cannot be bent to render even so charitable a verdict as this. Mao and Chou actively sought collaboration with capitalist governments and on more than one occasion openly concluded agreements with reactionary ruling classes against their own peoples. This has been most clearly documented since the Sino-Soviet split, when

Peking stepped out from under Moscow's umbrella and began to make its own way in the world.

The greatest single test of Maoism as a revolutionary doctrine and guide to action came in Indonesia.

In the early 1960s the Indonesian Communist Party (PKI) was the largest in the world that did not hold state power. In a country of 100 million people it claimed 3 million members plus a membership of 3 million more in its youth organization. An additional 20 million people belonged to trade unions and mass organizations under its leadership. No Communist Party in history ever had such a favorable numerical relationship of forces with which to wage a struggle for power. In the Sino-Soviet rupture, the PKI had sided with Peking.

Peking had to choose in Indonesia between the perspective of a worker-peasant revolution against the capitalist government of Sukarno, and the benefits of cultivating Sukarno's friendship and alliance. It pursued the latter course.

Instead of opposing Sukarno, the PKI, with Mao's endorsement, subordinated itself to the capitalist regime on the grounds that it was "anti-imperialist." In the decade before 1965, Sukarno placed steadily heavier restrictions on civil liberties and political rights, including dissolving the elected Constituent Assembly in 1959, and thereafter ruling by decree like an absolute monarch. In this he received the full support of the PKI. The motion to dissolve the assembly was made by none other than PKI Chairman D. N. Aidit! The class-collaborationist line of the PKI was put as bluntly as it could be in a speech by Aidit to the party's Central Committee in December 1961:

in carrying out our national struggle we must hold firmly to the basic principle: place the interests of class and of the Party below the national interest, that is, place the national interest above the interests of class and of the Party.[4]

In September 1965, when its bourgeois allies turned on it, the PKI was completely unprepared. Indonesia's generals were able to carry out one of the bloodiest massacres in history without even a semblance of opposition. By the end of 1966 the death toll stood somewhere between 500,000 and a million.

What happened in Indonesia was not the result of clever technical maneuvers—the element of surprise or of efficient military organization by the ruling class. The weakness of the PKI was not technical but political. It had educated the masses to look to the liberal section of the ruling class for leadership, to expect justice from the existing society, to believe that such extreme measures as those taken by the generals could not happen. The effect was to paralyze the masses' will to resist, to make them hope, even after the killing started, that things could be resolved—not by reacting in kind, but by passively waiting for the trouble to blow over. The result for the workers and peasants of Indonesia was a terrible historic tragedy that they are still paying for today. The conduct of the PKI, however, was not simply tragic. It was a criminal betrayal of the masses it led.

What was Peking's role in all of this, apart from its public alliance with Aidit? And what was its responsibility? It is plausible that the PKI formulated its line independently of Peking; and even that its support to Mao against Moscow was an act of opportunism. Mao's minimal obligation in that case was to say openly to the masses of Indonesia: Place no trust in your capitalist masters; when it comes to open battle, no quarter will be given.

But to say this would have meant losing the backing of Sukarno in China's efforts to gain recognition by capitalist governments. It would have meant a break with the PKI and the prestige it gave to the Maoist camp in the split with Moscow.

To the nationalist bureaucracy in Peking these considerations loomed larger than the fate of the Indonesian masses and their needed revolution. Peking published Sukarno's speeches in *Peking Review*—as contributions to Marxist theory. And on the forty-fifth anniversary of the PKI's founding, in May 1965, Mao offered a personal endorsement of its class-collaborationist course. In his message of greetings to the PKI Central Committee he said:

> The Central Committee of the Communist Party of Indonesia headed by Comrade D. N. Aidit has skillfully and creatively applied and developed Marxism-Leninism in the light of the revolutionary practice of its own country; it has Indonesianized Marxism-Leninism with outstanding success, independently worked out its revolutionary line and policies which conform to the basic interests of the Indonesian people, and led Indonesia's revolutionary struggle from victory to victory. The Communist Party of China is very proud to have such a close and staunch comrade-in-arms as the Communist Party of Indonesia.[5]

If anything has changed in the years since the Indonesian debacle, it is that Peking has no more mass parties in its camp to act as intermediaries in its relations with neocolonial administrations. This has brought its essential attitude toward these regimes into sharper focus. Another factor has been the "opening toward China" of American imperialism, first signaled by discussions in Warsaw in 1969. This gave Maoism its first opportunity since the onset of the cold war to do serious business with the leading superpower. And to show the world what it was willing to pay for the privilege.

Nineteen seventy-one was a watershed year in Peking's preparations for the détente with Washington that was soon to be consummated with Nixon's visit. Mao's principal concern was to demonstrate to the U.S. ruling class that the Chinese Communist Party was a party of order—as the French CP had done in its opposition to the French general strike of May–June 1968. The two sides of Mao's demonstration were to show that China would back existing "Third World" governments against their own peoples in a revolutionary crisis; and that it would bloc with imperialism against the Soviet Union.

In 1971 three major upheavals occurred in the colonial world: the nationalist rebellion of the Bengali people against the Urdu minority that dominated the government of Pakistan; the "youth rebellion" in Ceylon (later renamed Sri Lanka); and the showdown between the military dictatorship of the Sudan and the Sudanese trade unions and Communist Party. In each case, Mao sided demonstratively and publicly with the capitalist government against the mass movement.

After the 1962 China-India border war, China sought an alliance with Pakistan. To cement this alignment, Peking chose to refrain from any public criticism of Pakistan's military dictatorship. This meant refraining from offering support to the Bengali majority, whose oppression constituted a festering wound in that unhappy country.

Pakistan was not a country in any ordinary sense of the word. It was an artificial creation of British imperialism: two pieces of land separated by 1,000 miles of Indian territory. This "nation," created only in 1947 from parts of India, had no common language, history, or culture. The only basis of a common government was the fact that both parts contained people who professed the Muslim faith. Yet on that skimpy theocratic foundation the West Pakistanis proceeded to loot the Bengali-speaking East for more than two decades.

In March 1971, when General Yahya Khan set aside an election in which his supporters had been roundly defeated, the Bengali masses exploded in spontaneous revolution. Yahya responded with a genocidal bloodbath. Ultimately the people of "East Pakistan" won their fight, expelled their foreign rulers, and established the independent nation of Bangladesh. But Mao, in this conflict, stood not on the side of the oppressed but on the side of the oppressors. Chou En-lai spelled out China's position in a public letter to Yahya Khan of April 12, 1971:

> We are certain that, thanks to the contacts which you and your collaborators are increasing and thanks to all your efforts, the situation in Pakistan will be restored to normality. The unity of Pakistan and of the peoples of the eastern and western provinces of the country is essential to guarantee that the nation will survive and achieve prosperity and power. A distinction must be made between the great mass of the people and a handful of individuals intent on sabotaging Pakistan's unity.[6]

The situation was not restored to "normality." Two nations emerged from the civil war of 1971, in the process revealing that the ties that had briefly united them were coercive and not organic. The appeal to national unity, endorsed by Chou En-lai, was no more than the stock rationalization for national exploitation of every reactionary capitalist government. It is instructive here also to see the use made by Chou of the words "a handful of individuals," now a hackneyed phrase used in Peking to describe every group it does not like. In this case the "handful" proved to be the overwhelming majority of the population.

In Ceylon, the election of a liberal coalition government in 1970 had raised mass expectations of important social reforms. The capitalist government of Sirimavo Bandaranaike included as minority partners the pro-Moscow Communist Party and the renegade ex-Trotskyists of the Lanka Sama Samaja Party (LSSP). This had helped it to win votes from the workers and peasants of Ceylon, but made it difficult to secure imperialist investment and loans. In the spring of 1971, the coalition government sought to rectify this instability by dealing a demonstrative blow to the mass movement, thus reassuring world finance capital of its reliability. Peking, seeking to add Ceylon to its list of friendly governments, endorsed this piece of cynical brutality. On March 6, an attack was staged on the U.S. embassy in Colombo, attributed to a previously unheard of "Mao Youth Front." This is generally believed to have been staged by the government itself, or by the embassy staff.

On March 16, Bandaranaike declared a state of emergency and

began a crackdown on the mass radical youth organization, the Janatha Vimukthi Peramuna (JVP—People's Liberation Front). The government-influenced press manufactured stories of a youth rebellion that was supposed to be an armed conspiracy of the terrorist Left. On this trumped-up basis, arms and ammunition were solicited by the government from world imperialism—and from both Moscow and Peking—and a real campaign of government terror was unleashed against all forms of opposition.

In response to this government assault, the JVP mounted what resistance it could, and scattered fighting took place throughout the island for several weeks. Hundreds were arrested and held in detention camps, to be brought to trial only much later. The capitalist government used all of this to severely restrict civil liberties in Ceylon (Sri Lanka) thereafter.

Peking's intervention, apart from the open supply of arms, was to offer Ceylon a $30 million, interest-free loan on May 26, and to provide political cover for the repression of the Left. Chou En-lai again came to the rescue, with a telegram to Bandaranaike. In it he said in part:

> Following Chairman Mao Tsetung's teaching the Chinese people have all along opposed ultra "left" and right opportunism in their protracted revolutionary struggles.
>
> We are glad to see that thanks to the efforts of Your Excellency and the Ceylon Government, the chaotic situation created by a handful of persons who style themselves "Guevarists" and into whose ranks foreign spies have sneaked has been brought under control.
>
> We believe that as a result of Your Excellency's leadership and the cooperation and support of the Ceylonese people these acts of rebellion plotted by reactionaries at home and abroad for the purpose of undermining the interests of the Ceylonese people are bound to fail.
>
> We fully agree to the correct position of defending state sovereignty and guarding against foreign interference as referred to by Your Excellency.[7]

In July and August 1971, Peking offered support to General Nimeiry of the Sudan in his efforts to stamp out the pro-Moscow Sudanese Communist Party, as well as the trade unions, which the CP led. Nimeiry's campaign was carried out under the slogan of crushing all "Communists, traitors to the fatherland, and enemies of God." In August, Nimeiry sent a note of thanks to Mao and Chou En-lai for not criticizing his witch-hunts.[8]

The following February, Mao and Chou welcomed Nixon to Peking. Between then and his summit meeting in Moscow in May, Nixon began the bombing of Hanoi and mined the principal North Vietnamese harbor at Haiphong. As the Pentagon Papers later revealed, this step had been rejected for years by Washington policy makers out of the belief that it would inevitably lead to direct intervention in the Vietnam War by both Moscow and Peking. But by the spring of 1972, both Brezhnev and Mao had their sights on American aid and trade. They made no countermove to each escalation of the U.S. bombing of North Vietnam, leaving the embattled Vietnamese liberation fighters to their own devices. The two largest workers' states deserted the Vietnamese people under fire. The magnitude of this act is not reduced by the fact that the corrupt American puppet regime in South Vietnam was later vanquished.

Since 1972, Peking has become, outside of the right-wing fringe in American politics, the strongest proponent of strengthening NATO, of U.S. production of the neutron bomb, of the rearmament of Japan, and of the bolstering of reactionary military and dictatorial governments around the world. The only precondition is that these governments normalize diplomatic relations with China. Very few have refused to do so. Those regimes now on Peking's list of friendly powers—that is, immune from public criticism—include such unsavory outfits as Pinochet's junta in Chile, the Spanish monarchy, and the shah of Iran. If one lived in China today, one would never know that there are political prisoners, torture, and execution in Iran and Chile.

Peking's orientation in Mao's last year was perhaps best summed up by American author William Hinton, a Maoist of long standing and at that time chairman of the U.S.-China People's Friendship Association. In an interview Hinton explained that China now considered the Soviet Union, and not American imperialism, to be the main danger and was seeking common action with those capitalist politicians who shared this opinion. Said Hinton:

China judges world leaders by how well they understand this new relationship of forces. Thus they prefer [British Conservative Party leader Edward] Heath to [Labour Party leader Harold] Wilson, [West German right-winger Franz Josef] Strauss to [Social Democratic leader Willi] Brandt and [right-wing former U.S. Defense Secretary James] Schlesinger to Kissinger.[9]

This call for a worldwide alliance of ultraright, anticommunist politicians against the Soviet Union has more in common with the politics of cold war Washington than with the foreign policy of a government that claims to represent the interests of the workers and peasants.

Peking has even sought to create a special relationship with the ultraright wing of the American military establishment. On this score, witness the month-long red-carpet tour of China given to former U.S. Admiral Elmo R. Zumwalt in June-July 1977. Zumwalt gained fame as the commander of U.S. naval operations in Vietnam in 1968-70. His invitation to China was not based on the understandable need for Peking to have dealings with Washington, as Zumwalt no longer represented the U.S. government. He was there as a leader of the so-called Committee on the Present Danger, a group very little known in the U.S., but widely touted in the Peking press. This is a committee of right-wing militarists who criticize the U.S. government for being "soft on communism" and failing to spend enough money on bombs to meet the "Soviet threat." Its pronouncements, ignored by even the mainstream capitalist press, are dutifully reprinted in Peking.

Stalinism, in both its Chinese and Russian forms, expresses the narrow national interests and outlook of a privileged, petty-bourgeois social layer at the head of a workers' state. Such a formation can hold onto power through a bureaucratic machine only by excluding the working masses from political power. Its rigid authoritarianism reveals its actual weakness as a social grouping. It is here that the explanation of its affinity for Western imperialism must be sought. The bureaucracy is neither stable nor "at home" in the workers' state. Nor is it a new ruling class or a capitalist class in novel disguise. It neither represents the workers nor does it own the nationalized property. It plays no necessary role in the organization of production, as capitalist and precapitalist ruling classes have done. Its existence is parasitic.

Totalitarian regimes throughout history have been short-lived expressions of crisis, of extreme social tension (as distinguished from less extreme forms of class dictatorship, which have characterized the whole history of class society).

The mass expectations generated by the anticapitalist revolution and the elimination of the bulwarks of capitalist rule exacerbate the social tension between the masses and the emergent bureaucratic caste. Trotsky, describing this process in Stalin's Russia of the late 1930s, put it this way:

In the land that has gone through the proletarian revolution, it is impossible to foster inequality, create an aristocracy, and accumulate privileges save by bringing down upon the masses floods of lies and ever more monstrous repressions.

Embezzlement and theft, the bureaucracy's main sources of income, do not constitute a system of exploitation in the scientific sense of the term. But from the standpoint of the interests and position of the popular masses it is infinitely worse than any "organic" exploitation. The bureaucracy is not a possessing class, in the scientific sense of the term. But it contains within itself to a tenfold degree all the vices of a possessing class. It is precisely the absence of crystallized class relations and their very impossibility on the social foundation of the October Revolution that invest the working of the state machine with such a convulsive character. To perpetuate the systematic theft of the bureaucracy, its apparatus is compelled to resort to systematic acts of banditry. The sum total of all these things constitutes the system of Bonapartist gangsterism.[10]

The bureaucratic caste's lack of deep social roots in the productive process accounts both for the ferocity of its rule and its constant need to seek support from alien class forces for use against the workers. This is the basis of Stalinist class collaborationism with imperialism, a necessary condition for the bureaucracy's continued existence.

Domestically, the regime cultivates a relatively better off sector of the peasantry and whatever privileged layers are available in the cities as a counterweight to the workers and radical students, while internationally it seeks accommodation with imperialism or its satellites.

Imperialism—and this includes all the industrially advanced countries of Western Europe, Japan, and the United States—must in the long run maintain a position of irreconcilable hostility to the nationalized, planned economies of all the workers' states, since these exclude large-scale penetration by foreign capital. Its attitude toward the Stalinist bureaucracies at their head is more flexible. As long as imperialism lacks the short-run capability to restore capitalism, it will exploit the bureaucracies' need for imperialist "support" in order to choke off aid that the bureaucracies might feel pressured into granting to insurgent anticapitalist movements elsewhere, and to play Moscow and Peking against one another to the advantage of the capitalist West.

In the early years after the victory of the Chinese revolution, Washington's China policy was founded on the premise that the diplomatic, economic, and military blockade of Peking might lead the Chinese people to welcome the return of Chiang Kai-shek or that such an outcome could be imposed from outside without a major war. This proved to be a pipe dream. It finally became plain to Washington that the grievances the Chinese people had against Maoism would still never lead them to return voluntarily to capitalist rule. That put an end to any hopes in ruling

American circles of a quick or easy triumph over the Chinese revolution. Then came the windfall for Washington of the Sino-Soviet split. Washington's first inclination was to exploit this rupture through agreements with Moscow at China's expense. This produced the period of the most radical pronouncements on world affairs from the Chinese government. Over time, however, American imperialism reevaluated this one-sided strategy and decided to test whether its interests could not be better served by offering an opening to Mao as well for an understanding at the expense of the world revolution. This turn was prompted by setbacks to the U.S. expeditionary force in Vietnam following the Tet offensive in 1968. Diplomatic channels were then opened for indirect discussions with Peking in Warsaw. The Mao regime adopted a cooperative posture. After Peking's intentions were tested in Vietnam, Washington's tactical turn was completed with the Nixon-Kissinger overtures to China for a détente agreement.

Peking's eagerness to play Washington's game has proven immensely advantageous for American imperialism. In exchange for a seat in the United Nations and expanded opportunities for trade with the U.S., Western Europe, and Japan, Peking has dropped its calls for "people's war" against colonialist domination. (The only real exceptions are against the thoroughly discredited colonial-settler states—Rhodesia, South Africa, Israel, and Northern Ireland—and in some of the few remaining direct colonies. Moscow and even some bourgeois liberals take the same stand.)

Both Moscow and Peking have provided a pitiful spectacle of "socialist" hares trying to run with the imperialist hounds. Much of their diplomacy today is devoted to warning this or that capitalist government against the schemes of its opponent. During the last days of the Vietnam War, for example, the Soviet Union began circulating an undoubtedly fictitious quote from Mao in which he is alleged to have told a 1965 CCP Politburo meeting, "We must definitely secure for ourselves Southeast Asia, including South Vietnam, Thailand, Burma, Malaysia and Singapore."[11]

Peking has responded in kind by calling on the neocolonial regimes of the world to brand the Soviet Union imperialist—and a "greater danger" than the United States to boot. Here, at least, there do not appear to be any serious differences of opinion between the Mao group and its successors. After the purge of the "gang of four" the Peking *People's Daily* wrote of the regime in the Soviet Union:

This new upstart in the ranks of imperialism is bound to carry out an all-round aggression and expansion against the Third World with tenfold of voracity and hundredfold of madness. Through their experiences of struggles in many years, the Third World countries and their peoples have come to realize more and more clearly that Soviet social-imperialism has gone farther than old-line imperialism in its aggression and expansion abroad and is their most dangerous enemy.[12]

Hua Kuo-feng has stated virtually openly that this line means support to the military dictatorships of Latin America against Cuba. In a friendly review of an article entitled "Soviet Strategic Triangle Threatens Latin America" in the right-wing Argentine magazine *Review of the River Plate,* reflecting the anti-communist propaganda of the Argentine military regime, Hsin-hua wrote:

The article says that the open intervention of Cuban armed forces in Angola, masterminded by the Soviet Union, has led the countries of the American continent to reconsider the advisability of taking some kind of preventive measures to preclude future acts of Soviet aggression that use the armed forces of a third country as mercenaries.[13]

Such appeals are directed first of all to the U.S. State Department. They are meant to impress on capitalist policy makers that Peking is a reliable ally against other workers' states and against potential revolutionary actions of the masses anywhere else. In exchange for this truckling to counterrevolution, Peking hopes to win some trade and possibly some diplomatic and armament support from the United States, Western Europe, and Japan, so the bureaucracy can continue to build "socialism" behind its new version of the Great Wall.

But can we leave matters there? Does Peking have any alternative other than to seek aid from imperialism? Obviously the Chinese government should not turn down favorable trade agreements with any government, capitalist or not. It may even have to pay dearly for the "privilege" of doing business with foreign capitalist governments and corporations. This is not at issue.

The question is: What road out of impoverishment actually stands before the Chinese people? Does it lie through encouraging national isolation, and allying with the enemies of socialism throughout the world against the movements of the working class? This kind of cynicism cannot be justified, even on the grounds that it is realistic or productive. In addition to the moral abhorrence of such conduct for anyone who favors the emancipation of humanity from class oppression, it simply does not and cannot work. And the Stalinists are not so stupid that they do not know this. They choose the path of alliance with foreign capitalism because on some level they know that the expansion of the world socialist revolution and the achievement of a society of genuine human freedom would leave no place for them.

Marx's conception of socialism, as an international society founded on the democratic rule of the associated producers, remains more realistic and practical than all the shady dealings and brutalities of the Stalinist bureaucrats. Its realism can be seen in the periodic irrepressible explosions of the oppressed in every continent, seeking even without organization and leadership to win for themselves the right to control their own destinies.

These were the concepts that guided the leaders of the first workers' state before the advent of the Stalinist degeneration. Internally, the Soviet Union was founded on the democratic control of the state and the economy by the soviets, the workers' councils, where all the political tendencies of the Russian working class and the workers of the other nationalities of the Soviet Union debated their contending programs and involved the masses in real political life. Internationally, the very conception of the Soviet Union stood in stark opposition to the notion of socialism in one country—because it was not meant to be a solitary country at all, but a world government in embryo.

The Soviet constitution of Lenin's day established a state structure not for a single isolated country, but for a federation of nations with a common government and economy. The Soviet *Union* was established with provisions for new countries joining the union—as well as the right of secession of its member states in the event that disagreements made them feel the need to withdraw for a period of time.

One of the highest priorities of the young Soviet Union, in reality its very highest, was to aid working class battles in other countries. This was not looked on as an altruistic charity. It was not regarded as some kind of left-wing Red Cross activity, the way radicals influenced by liberalism and Stalinism today tend to see support to "foreign" struggles. It was taken as part of a common battle that would culminate in a united world society.

Compare the internationalism of Lenin and Trotsky—and the Marxist strategy for economic development that flows from it—to the hidebound national chauvinism of every one of the Stalinist-controlled states of today. China's very constitution provides for a single, unitary, permanent nation-state and does not conceive of unification with other countries in a common economic entity.

Such a perspective assumes a life-span for capitalism of generations, left to its own devices outside of the one country where "socialism" is being built.

The pervasive nationalism of China's Stalinist ruling caste is an injustice not only to the international needs of the Chinese revolution; it also denies the national rights of China's non-Chinese minorities. These peoples, while comprising only 6 percent of the population, some 54 millions, occupy the vast majority of China's territory—the sparsely settled grasslands and steppes of Inner Mongolia, Chinese Turkestan, and Tibet. The present stand of the CCP on the national rights of these minority peoples is actually a retreat from the positions on which the CCP was founded. As late as 1931 in the constitution of the "Kiangsi Soviet Republic," the CCP's rural guerrilla enclave, it was stated:

The Soviet Government of China recognizes the right of self-determination of the national minorities in China, their right to complete separation from China and to the formation of an independent state for each national minority. All Mongolians, Tibetans, Miao, Yao, Koreans and others living on the territory of China shall enjoy full right of self-determination, i.e., they may either join the Union of Chinese Soviets or secede from it and form their own state as they may prefer.[14]

In contrast to this Leninist position, the present constitution of China, adopted in March 1978, declares:

The People's Republic of China is a unitary multi-national state. . . . acts which undermine the unity of the nationalities are prohibited. . . . All the national autonomous areas are inalienable parts of the People's Republic of China.[15]

Foreign policy for a workers' state cannot be limited to governmental relations with foreign and internal nations. There is also the question of the Chinese Communist Party's own international actions. Has the CCP sought to unify revolutionary workers' organizations around the world into a common bloc in the struggle against world capitalism? Surely this is one of the most pressing tasks of revolutionists, and an indispensable one if experiences are to be shared, national parochialism avoided, and a common political line of conduct hammered out.

In the first years of the Sino-Soviet split it did look briefly as though the CCP was contemplating the creation of an international organization of "Marxist-Leninist parties." This enterprise was dropped completely after the Indonesian debacle and the beginning of the Cultural Revolution. In Mao's last years, Peking showed not the slightest interest in the Maoists outside China. When the Chinese press reprinted articles from these groups they virtually never chose material concerning the class struggle in their own countries but confined their selection to messages of congratulations to Peking on important holidays and denunciations of the Soviet regime. In the United States, for example, Peking allowed many years to go by before bothering to select a replacement from among the contending Maoist groups for the defection of the Progressive Labor Party in the late 1960s. A slight shift appears to have been made on this front by the more outward-looking Hua-Teng team, signaled by the invitation of Michael Klonsky of the small U.S. Communist Party (Marxist-Leninist) to Peking in the summer of 1977, a visit that was given front-page treatment in the *People's Daily*.

11. The "Two-Line Struggle"

There has been broad agreement within the CCP leadership on the general outlines of China's foreign policy. Differences between the Mao faction and its successors, or between Mao and figures such as Liu Shao-ch'i and Lin Piao, have only been hinted at and seem to revolve principally around Peking's relations with the Soviet Union. The same is not true of domestic policy, where the question of the bureaucracy's continued ability to rule is more immediately posed.

China's post-Mao leaders have renounced the main slogans and campaigns of Mao's Cultural Revolution, just as Mao had previously rejected elements of the USSR's pattern of priorities and organization ten years earlier. To make sense of the new change of line in Peking it is necessary to probe what actually lies behind the highly abstract slogans under which it has been carried out. This means sorting out the issues in the Cultural Revolution that were presented by the Maoists at the time as a "two-line struggle" between Mao's "proletarian revolutionary line" and the "capitalist-roaders."

The most important of the issues in this war of words was the battle between what Mao called "politics in command" as opposed to the line of Liu Shao-ch'i and Teng Hsiao-p'ing, which Mao dubbed "production in command." A parallel dispute took place over the relative priority of being "red," that is, politically committed to the party's current line and leadership, versus being "expert" in economic, technical, or scientific work.

Let us first examine the claims made by the Maoists themselves for the significance of these differences. The most elaborate theory has been developed over a number of years by Paul Sweezy, a well-known American Marxist economist and an editor of *Monthly Review* magazine, in collaboration with French Marxist economist Charles Bettelheim. Sweezy in his youth rallied to the cause of socialism, which he first came to identify with the Stalinist leadership of the Soviet Union. After the Khrushchev revelations and the Sino-Soviet split he became disillusioned with Moscow and shifted his loyalty to Peking. For Sweezy the problem was to prove that there was a fundamental difference between his new loyalty and everything that had disappointed him in Moscow Stalinism. This essential distinction, he came to argue after the Cultural Revolution, was that in China there was mass participation, while in Russia the party leaders were concerned only with economic performance.

In a special 1974 issue of *Monthly Review* devoted to a balance sheet of the last twenty-five years of the Marxist movement, Sweezy professed to see "a renaissance of Marxism" which he said had been "accomplished through the powerful polemic directed by the Chinese at the Moscow-oriented Communist movement in the early 1960s."[1] Sweezy wrote:

In repudiating the Soviet model, the Chinese had necessarily to strike out in other directions. The term which most effectively summarizes this course, partly new and partly a shifting of emphasis, is "putting politics in command" as contrasted to the capitalist *and* Soviet practice of putting economics in command. This is not the place to spell out the meaning of putting politics in command: suffice it to say that its central core is egalitarianism in the widest and deepest sense of the term, i.e., the reduction and ultimate elimination not only of differences in income, but also of differences in knowledge, power, privilege, and everything else that divides people and sets them against each other, either as groups or as individuals, and thus makes it impossible for them to live together in solidarity and happiness.[2]

Thus, for Sweezy, the source of bureaucratic degeneration after a successful socialist revolution is reduced to one thing: a one-sided concern for industrialization without sufficient politicalization of the masses. Applying this yardstick to the Cultural Revolution in China, he later wrote:

There is little doubt that a bureaucratic ruling stratum was growing and consolidating its power in China during the 1950's and early 1960's. By 1966 it seems clear that it already had a majority in the Central Committee of the Communist Party and occupied most of the decisive posts in the central and regional administrations. Most likely it would have soon moved in the direction of capitalism already pioneered by the Eastern European countries. But Mao and a small group of faithful followers refused to acquiesce in this retrogression. Using the at least partly spontaneous Red Guard movement as their initial weapon, they launched the Cultural Revolution, roused the masses, unseated the bureaucratic leaders, and in this way insured that China would continue on the road to socialism. . . .[3]

This account is quite off course, but there is one correct point in it: the administrative methods and priorities of the CCP leadership until the Great Leap Forward of 1958-59, and again in the years just before Mao launched the Cultural Revolution at the end of 1965, were closely copied from the Soviet regime. Chapter 10 took up Peking's differences with the USSR in foreign policy after the public rupture in 1960. In domestic affairs, however, the entire governmental apparatus, from the mechanisms of economic planning to the political police, was created after 1949 under the tutelage of Russian advisers.

These policies have long been familiar to revolutionary Marxists. They are the expression in the Soviet Union and Eastern Europe of•the rule of a conservative and privileged bureaucratic caste, a distinct petty-bourgeois social formation that excludes the masses of working people from any decision-making power. They are best described in Leon Trotsky's 1936 work *The Revolution Betrayed*, which lays bare the material interests that the Stalinist ruling group defends and the repressive measures that it must use to preserve its regime from challenges by the working class.

Mao was wrong to brand this system—more accurately, certain secondary and incidental features of it—as "capitalism." Neither in the Soviet Union under Khrushchev and Brezhnev nor in China before the Cultural Revolution had the reactionary bureaucracy created the essential preconditions for a reversion to capitalist society. There is no class of people who own, as individuals, private blocs of capital. The principal means of production—factories, mines, transport—as well as trade and finance remain state property. Individuals cannot buy factories, cannot accumulate capital, cannot hire workers for their own personal gain. Production goals are decided by state agencies on the basis of supplying particular needs, not on the basis of the blind increase in profits as under capitalism. This remains true no matter how arbitrarily those decisions are arrived at under the bureaucracy or how inefficiently they are carried out.

Apart from his use of the false label "capitalism," Mao criticized certain specific policies of the Soviet government under Khrushchev and of his own colleagues in the CCP hierarchy. He singled out the widespread political apathy of the mass of Russian workers as a danger to socialism. Mao in turn identified socialism with the unchallenged rule of his party, his faction, and, ultimately, his person. He came to identify the sources of that apathy in the concessions made by Moscow to the objective needs of industrialization. The training of a generation of skilled workers, the education of a layer of qualified scientists and technicians, the decision by Russian censors after the death of Stalin to permit a wider range of foreign and domestic literature—all came to be viewed by Mao as sources of hostile ideas that could undermine the authority of the party.

There was, of course, some truth to this. Trotsky had explained the rise of Stalinism in the Soviet Union by the country's industrial backwardness, the relatively small size of its working class (compared to the peasantry), the general low level of culture, material scarcity, and international isolation. The growth of a powerful, educated, and skilled working class is a threat to the bureaucracy, but not, as Mao claimed, because the workers become imbued with bourgeois ideas. The increase in urbanization, proletarianization, and the general rise in the material standard of living and of culture deepen the objective contradictions between the working class and the bureaucracy and increase the social weight of the workers for the coming antibureaucratic revolution.

The Russian Communist Party and the Mao faction of the Chinese Communist Party confronted this challenge in different ways. Moscow took the risk of establishing the educational institutions necessary for an industrially advanced society. The Soviet bureaucracy's calculation has been to combine minimal material concessions to the workers—disparaged by Mao as "goulash communism"—with selective repression by the secret police. It has largely abandoned the efforts of the Stalin era to control the thoughts and movements of every individual citizen, at least if they keep their thoughts to themselves.

Moscow paid a price for this course, both in the Soviet Union and in the bloc of East European countries it dominates. It is difficult to maintain the fiction that the party hierarchy is a revolutionary group. The bureaucracy lives in isolation from the working class, an obvious elitist hierarchy that moves in its own world of relative wealth and privilege. The range of ideas permitted to Soviet and East European scientists and writers was not supposed to include the right to dissent on political questions. But it has, in fact, led to pockets of conscious opposition. Sometimes this has flared into the open as in the Hungarian revolution of 1956 or the Prague Spring of 1968.

(These challenges prompted the bureaucracy to take back some of the concessions it had grudgingly permitted. But up to the present this tightening up has not gone so far as a return to the wholesale terror and obscurantism of the Stalin years.)

It is not surprising that Mao could raise a revolt against the Chinese proponents of this repellant and ossified system. Using slogans such as "To Rebel Is Justified," involving the masses in "politics," and crusading against bureaucracy, privilege, and "bourgeois" ideas, Mao was able in 1966-68 to defeat the majority of the old-line CCP functionaries and establish the dominance of his own faction, represented by the now-disgraced "gang of four."

If the first line in this "two-line struggle" holds no mysteries, the same is not true of Mao's perspective. Mao was a different story, not only because of the radical-sounding slogans he raised but also because his central method consisted of mass mobilization. It was this characteristic that won most of the attention in the West and gave rise to the endless stream of books and articles by foreign visitors in the late 1960s and early 1970s, describing an almost uncanny degree of political involvement, solidarity, and unanimity of the Chinese people.

Maoism as a distinct ideological current within the Stalinist camp existed only in embryo prior to the Great Leap Forward of 1958. It emerged at that time in response to two complementary challenges to bureaucratic rule: the inability of the regime to secure control over the peasants' grain, and a radicalization of the urban intellectuals and workers.

Before it came to power in 1949, the CCP in its rural military bases had assiduously sought the support of the well-to-do section of the peasantry. From 1937 on, it had even dropped the slogan of land reform from its program as part of its efforts to enter a coalition government with Chiang Kai-shek.

This policy created a serious problem after 1949, which the belated land reform alone did not solve. The peasants had been educated by the CCP to expect from the revolution nothing more than a renovated Chinese capitalism, promoted in party literature as New Democracy. With the shift of tens of thousands of party cadres from the countryside into the cities the peasants began to quietly assert their own idea of what the revolution had been all about by raising their own standard of living. Grain was withheld from the party's collectors. The importation of Stalin's economic policies exacerbated this problem by placing overwhelming emphasis on heavy industry. This deprived the state-owned economy of the consumer goods that it could have used to win the loyalty of the peasants by offering something of value in exchange for their grain. In 1955 there was an actual grain crisis in which hunger reappeared in the cities. This jolted the regime into an attempt to repeat Stalin's remedy of forced collectivization. In China as in Russia the peasant collectivization had not only a bureaucratic but also a utopian character, because it was not accompanied by any real improvement in the productive forces of agriculture, either in mechanization or in the provision of fertilizer.

In effect, while collectivization was presented as a means of long-term improvement in the productivity of agriculture, it became a more and more frantic short-term scramble to find administrative means simply to lay hands on the peasants' produce. This is plain from the frenetic changes in the goals and pace of collectivization between 1955 and 1958. On July 30, 1955, the First Five-Year Plan was submitted to the National People's Congress for approval. That this was a mere formality may be judged from the fact that the plan had begun in 1953 and was already half completed before being voted on by China's elected government. The congress resolution projected that by the end of 1957, "about one third of all the peasant households in the country will have joined the present agricultural producers' cooperatives of elementary form."[4]

Yet twenty-four hours after the congress adjourned, Mao personally overrode its decisions, calling a meeting of regional party secretaries where he ordered the immediate wholesale collectivization of agriculture. In June of 1955 only 14 percent of peasant households were organized in agricultural producers' cooperatives. By December this had jumped to 63 percent and in 1956 all individual title to land was abolished, with collectivization reaching 98 percent of peasant families by 1957.[5]

This still failed to have the results the government wanted. The collectives were contiguous with the old villages, and family and clan ties were strong enough for the collectives to put their own interests ahead of the state's grain quotas. The CCP faced a classical "scissors crisis," first analyzed by Trotsky in the Soviet Union of the 1920s, in which the perceived interests of the peasants and workers were moving apart like the blades of an opening scissors. Sales of agricultural produce to the state stagnated from 1955 to 1956 and increased only marginally in 1957.[6]

The bureaucracy, in the habit of commanding, and constitutionally incapable of involving the masses in economic planning, proceeded to act on the illusion of its own omnipotence. It was at this point that Mao proposed an ideological and administrative solution to economic and social problems: the adventure of the People's Communes.

China's agricultural crisis occurred at the same time as the debate within the world Stalinist movement over the Stalin question. At root this was a dispute over the degree of totalitarianism that was indispensable for the survival of the bureaucratic caste. Khrushchev, seeking to bolster a weakened party center by making concessions to the Russian masses, had denounced Stalin at the beginning of 1956. In the fall of that year the Hungarian revolution shook the capitals of all the bureaucratized workers' states.

In May–June 1957, Peking initiated its attempt to carry out the international line, in the brief thaw heralded by the slogan, "Let a Hundred Flowers Bloom, Let a Hundred Schools of Thought Contend." As in previous "mass" campaigns, meetings were held throughout China, this time to invite criticism of the regime's shortcomings and abuses. But much to the government's dismay, tens of thousands of students, intellectuals, and workers began to denounce real abuses and not imaginary ones. Some even went so far as to call for a new, Leninist party, the establishment of democracy, and the abolition of special privilege.

This episode soured the CCP leadership on any more unstructured experiments in mass expression. In the "antirightist" campaign of the fall of 1957, many thousands of people who had dared to speak out were fired from their jobs and deported to remote areas of the countryside for "thought reform."

It was these expressions of genuine social struggle threatening its rule that convinced the bureaucracy to venture into uncharted waters in trying to bring the masses under control. In the Great Leap Forward many of the later typical schemes of Mao achieved prominence for the first time. These included the involvement of the entire population in study and self-criticism circles where they were required to profess their faith in the party leadership. Here mental reservations—not to speak of actual opposition—could be discovered early and struggled against. This was the creation of "collectivist man" with a vengeance.

Accompanying this campaign was a drive to extract extra unpaid labor through moral exhortations, in a climate where refusal was tantamount to being branded a counterrevolutionary. Certain other distinctly Maoist ideas were also floated in 1958-59:

hostility to intellectuals, schools, and knowledge; a distrust of things urban and things foreign; a romantic idealization of peasant life, stressing its conformity, hard work, and obedience, all pointedly counterposed to the volatile and critical habits of city workers and intellectuals.

In a sense, Mao's ideas were logical enough from the standpoint of preserving the rule of the bureaucracy. But what they revealed was the bureaucracy's basic incompatibility with the most elementary requirements of developing a socialist society, or even a modern industry. The CCP found itself in conflict with the basic drives of socialism: an international outlook, the goal of a world socialist society, the need for genuine democratic control over the workers' state, the need for knowledge and culture. This more than anything else revealed the essentially nonproletarian character of China's ruling stratum, no matter how loudly or frequently it invoked Marxism-Leninism-Mao Tsetung Thought.

Mao's innovations meant devoting incalculable amounts of time in every factory, school, and commune to the regulation of individual behavior. Maoism came to include an open hostility to all ideas that could challenge its own unique authority, even the established ideas of science and technology. (Soviet Stalinism had gone through something similar to this in its efforts in the dismal period of the late 1940s to have ignorant party hacks deduce from "Marxist" first principles the correct positions in biology and physics.)

What Mao and his supporters conceived of as a spur to workers' productivity, under the ideological lash of the party, produced its own crisis. The Great Leap proved to be an unmitigated disaster. The peasants responded to the new regimentation with what amounted to a sit-down strike. In the cities the workers simply refused to participate in urban communes, and these were soon abandoned. The harvest of grain in 1958, planted before the communes were organized, was a record 207 million tons. In 1959 it fell to 163 million tons and continued downward in 1960.

In industry, the party cadres tried to carry out their instructions in a frenzy of overfulfilling quotas. Without a democratically determined plan, supplies were disrupted, machinery was speeded up to the breaking point, and exhaustion of the industrial workers set in, followed by a drastic decline in industrial output.

It was this harsh intervention of material reality that provoked the first serious rift in the CCP leadership. The origins of the "two-line struggle" can be traced to the Lushan plenum of the CCP Central Committee in July-August 1959. There the Great

Leap Forward and the "politics in command" line were attacked by P'eng Te-huai, the minister of defense, who had commanded the Chinese forces in the Korean War. He denounced the Great Leap as "petty-bourgeois fanaticism" and argued that "putting politics in command is no substitute for economic principles."[7]

The plenum arrived at a compromise. P'eng was purged, but most of the distinctive policies of the Great Leap were abandoned or de-emphasized. The communes continued in name, but effectively the decision-making units were thereafter the production brigades, that is, the old villages; the authority of the commune administration was sharply reduced.

The Cultural Revolution marked Mao's attempt to reassert the line of the Great Leap. That he had to crush virtually the whole of the old administrative apparatus in order to succeed in this is an indication of how badly burned the bureaucracy had been in 1958-59. That he *could* succeed in this enterprise was a measure of the bureaucracy's inability to propose a viable alternative policy or to resolve its internal disputes without recourse to the authority of a Stalinist pope.

The "two-line struggle" was never a fight between different classes, as the Maoists maintain. Nor were the most fundamental premises of Stalinism ever in dispute. Both sides defended the idea of the monolithic authority of the party, not only against other working class tendencies but against the party's members as well. Both supported the myth of building socialism in national isolation, and considered it a matter of course to offer political support to foreign capitalist governments that were prepared to do business with Peking. Both protected the privileges of the hierarchy and sought to enlarge them at the expense of the masses, although the Mao faction for a time effectively exploited popular discontent on this issue to deal blows to its factional rivals.

The distinctive ideas of Mao do not derive from Marxism at all, but from long-standing tendencies in Chinese politics going back to the last century, and even earlier. The terminology of the Western press is misleading in labeling the contending factions radicals and moderates. Other terms are more useful in capturing the essence of this fight. At the end of the nineteenth century, Chinese nationalists were split between traditionalists and Westernizers. While the fight in the CCP hierarchy takes place in a different period and in a society grounded on different social relations, it echoes in many ways that old dispute. The Liu Shao-ch'is and Teng Hsiao-p'ings have about them something of the typical modern bureaucrat, infused with the belief in the power of command structures, of technology, of modern, high-power ways of getting things done. They are more reflective in that respect of the typical functionary today in Eastern Europe or the Soviet Union, or of the Western-looking reformers within the Chinese ruling class bureaucracy in the last years of the empire.

Mao on the other hand reflected the traditional xenophobia of the majority of China's old ruling class and of the peasantry. Few accusations could be more damaging to a Stalinist official in Mao's last years than to charge him with worshipping foreign things. Foreigners themselves, unless they came as the emissaries of powerful governments or from the ranks of the Maoist faithful, were not welcome in China.

Marxism from its inception has been both a revolutionary movement and a revolutionary science of society, a union of theory and practice. The writings of its outstanding leaders, from Marx and Engels to Lenin and Trotsky, are imbued with the need for serious theoretical study and the education of the mass of the oppressed to consciousness of the world that surrounds them. Mao Tsetung struck a very different note. For example, in a speech to a conference on education in 1964 he said:

We shouldn't read too many books. We should read Marxist books, but not too many of them either. It will be enough to read a dozen or so. . . .
   If you read too many books, they petrify your mind in the end. Emperor Wu of the Liang dynasty did pretty well in his early years, but afterwards he read many books, and didn't make out so well any more.[8]

This may seem to stand opposed not only to the Marxist attitude toward learning but even to the traditional Confucian reverence for the scholar-official. That is true, but China's rich culture provides more than one school of traditional thought. Mao's comments here are strongly reminiscent of the authoritarian and anti-intellectual Legalist school of philosophers, whose first powerful champion was China's first tyrant emperor, Ch'in Shih Hwang. Ch'in was one of Mao's personal heroes, to whom he compared himself in his 1948 poem "Snow."

Another idea of the Legalists that Mao shared was a distrust of cities and of urban life. This is a frequent theme in Mao's speeches and writings. One of his most explicit statements on this subject came in his address to the First Plenum of the Ninth Central Committee of the CCP in April 1969, where he sought to sum up and explain the causes of the "revisionism" of the Liu

Shao-ch'i–Teng Hsiao-p'ing faction. Things had been better, he said, in the days of rural guerrilla warfare.

Now we have entered the cities. This is a good thing. If we hadn't entered the cities Chiang Kai-shek would be occupying them. But it is also a bad thing because it caused our Party to deteriorate.[9]

The corrupting centers of industry and modernity pointed to by Mao are the home of the Chinese proletariat. Mao here revealed perhaps more than he intended about his real relationship with the class he claimed to represent.

Political loyalty for the Mao faction was not merely obeying orders given by the political machine, but personal, almost religious devotion to the leader. Here there is a direct parallel with the Stalin cult at its height. But there is also an element of the old emperor system as well, resurrected to serve the purposes of another regime based on minority rule. The emperor ruled not by any temporal mandate that could be withdrawn by the people, but by the mandate of heaven. Citizens were required to acknowledge his divinity as well as his legal authority.

These elements of the reactionary Chinese political tradition must be reconciled with the rejection of old cultural influences, as alleged by Mao's supporters. Jean Daubier, for example, writes:

The third goal set by the Cultural Revolution [in addition to defeating Liu Shao-ch'i and bringing the Red Guard youth into action under Mao's leadership] was to assure the supremacy of the Maoist ideology over revisionism. I have explained that this meant an enormous effort of politicization and ideological education, leading to the extirpation of individualism and the routing of traditional cultural and social influences. I have explained how, in the eyes of Mao, socialism—collectivist in its essence—is irreconcilable with individualism, the taste for personal possessions, the egocentric conception of the world. Hence the objective of remolding the mentality of men, of creating the total collectivist man.[10]

Mao's iconoclasm was most evident in the book burnings documented by his successors. These went beyond mere anti-intellectualism and constituted an attempt to abolish previous history and culture, to restrict the knowledge of the Chinese people to what the Mao government chose to tell them.

But this concept is itself the oldest of China's authoritarian, ruling class traditions. Ch'in Shih Hwang, as the Maoist press often pointed out approvingly, had the ambition to have history begin with his reign. To that end he built the Great Wall and burned the books of those who came before him. His attempt to destroy the memory of history failed. Mao, reflecting the grandiose aspirations of the petty-bourgeois caste he came to lead, became possessed of a similar ambition. He too sought to shut off China from the rest of the world and to burn the books and destroy the temples of the past.

Jean Daubier poses the "extirpation of individualism" as a goal of socialism. If what is meant by that is the struggle for human solidarity and the end of capitalist selfishness, his words are at best badly chosen. Marx's anger at capitalist exploitation was not limited to the theft of the workers' time and property—the accumulation by the capitalist of unpaid surplus-value. Marx counted our epoch as still part of the prehistory of humanity, in which we are not yet fully human, because of the exclusion of the great mass of the producers from the culture, science, and knowledge that could develop their individual capacities. That this could be accomplished only collectively Marx had no doubt. But he was scornful of those who sought to destroy the system of private property only to replace it with a state that would seek to extirpate talent and culture and reduce all people to the status of uneducated workers. To this he counterposed the appropriation of science and culture by everyone in a classless society.

In the next chapter we will come to the treatment of science and culture under the Mao regime. It is important first to examine some of the implications of Mao's course for a society claiming to be socialist. The effects of the Maoist propaganda machine have been pervasive on this score. Even outside of China many Western socialists have accepted, at least in part, that the Maoist assault on individuality, higher education, book learning, and the arts has been a defense of China's oppressed masses against a historically privileged elite; or, at the least, that the effects of these campaigns hurt only a small sector of Chinese society—the intellectuals.

Marx, in one of his earliest works, *The Economic and Philosophic Manuscripts of 1844,* discussed what he called "vulgar communism." This, of course, was before the advent of Stalinism, and he envisaged vulgar communism, if it were possible at all, as at least egalitarian, not dominated by a new privileged social stratum as in China and the Soviet Union. Marx wrote of such a system:

It wants to disregard talent, etc., in an *arbitrary* manner. For it the sole purpose of life and existence is direct, physical *possession.* The category of the *worker* is not done away with, but extended to all men. . . . This type of communism—since it negates the *personality* of man in every sphere—is but the logical expression of private property. . . . How little this annulment of private property is really an appropriation is in fact proved by the abstract negation of the entire world of culture and civilisation, the regression to the *unnatural* simplicity of the *poor* and crude man who has few needs and who has not only failed to go beyond private property, but has not yet even reached it.[11]

Marx held to these views throughout his life. In the *Grundrisse,* written in 1857-58 in preparation for his great work *Capital,* he discussed the nature of work under socialism and its relationship to leisure time. He took up the idea of the famous French utopian socialist Charles Fourier that work would become like play in a collectivist society where everyone collaborated for the common good. Marx disagreed. The nature of work would be changed, yes, and would become more enjoyable. But more important for Marx, the development of the productive forces would result in a saving of labor time, the shortening of the work day, which would make possible the flowering of people's talents and abilities in their free time, that is, their individuality. Marx wrote:

The saving of labour time [is] equal to an increase of free time, i.e., time for the full development of the individual, which in turn reacts back upon the productive power of labour as itself the greatest productive power. . . . Free time—which is both idle time and time for higher activity—has naturally transformed its possessor into a different subject, and he then enters into the direct production process as this different subject. This process is then both discipline, as regards the human being in the process of becoming; and, at the same time, practice, experimental science, materially creative and objectifying science, as regards the human being who has become, in whose head exists the accumulated knowledge of society.[12]

This humanist and universalist attitude toward individuality, science, and culture was shared by Lenin and the Bolsheviks. They advocated the fusion of political life and formal education, and the use of Soviet educational institutions to consciously combat bourgeois ideology and habits of slavishness. But this process carried out by a revolutionary workers' government bore little resemblance to the Maoist caricature. For Mao, even reading too many Marxist books is unhealthy for workers. For Lenin, Marxists works alone were not nearly enough. He advocated the publication in the USSR of the works of the French Enlightenment for their trenchant criticism of religion. In 1922 he wrote:

It would be the biggest and most grievous mistake a Marxist could make to think that the millions of the people (especially the peasants and artisans), who have been condemned by all modern society to darkness, ignorance and superstition, can extricate themselves from this darkness only along the straight line of a purely Marxist education. These masses should be supplied with the most varied atheist propaganda material, they should be made familiar with facts from the most diverse spheres of life, they should be approached in every possible way, so as to interest them, rouse them from their religious torpor, stir them from the most varied angles and by the most varied methods, and so forth.

The keen, vivacious and talented writings of the old eighteenth-century atheists wittily and openly attacked the prevailing clericalism and will very often prove a thousand times more suitable for arousing people from their religious torpor than the dull and dry paraphrases of Marxism. . . .[13]

In the same article, Lenin discussed the relationship between communism and scientists. He wrote:

In addition to the alliance with consistent materialists who do not belong to the Communist Party, of no less and perhaps even of more importance for the work which militant materialism should perform is an alliance with those modern natural scientists who incline towards materialism and are not afraid to defend and preach it as against the modish philosophical wanderings into idealism and scepticism which are prevalent in so-called educated society.

. . . Unless . . . the problems raised by the recent revolution in natural science are followed, and unless natural scientists are enlisted in the work of a philosophical journal, militant materialism can be neither militant nor materialism.[14]

For Marxists, the development of individuality, the mass dissemination of the best of old and new culture, the freedom of art, and the involvement of professional scientists in the elaboration of serious theoretical work are all integral parts of the creation of a genuine socialist society. Mao rejected all of these in the name of "proletarian politics"—a doctrine that in his hands proved to be neither proletarian in the interests it defended, nor political, insofar as it did not give the masses political rights but simply arrogated to Mao himself the right to make all important political decisions.

In all of this, Mao might emerge as an antihumanist Marxist, a populist leveller, or some kind of latter-day Cromwell or Calvin— were it not for the hypocrisy of the bureaucratic caste and its leader. That is what reveals this dispute between Marxism and Maoism to be more than a theoretical difference over methods of building socialism and exposes it as a struggle between hostile social groupings. Everyone was to be driven down to the level of an ordinary worker or peasant—except the bureaucratic hierarchy, with its servants, cooks, and expense accounts. No one was to read anything but party-approved materials—except the top echelons, for whom everything was available. Individualism was to be ruthlessly crushed among ordinary citizens—and the proof that one no longer had an "egocentric conception of the world" was that they joined unstintingly in the praise of Mao's personal genius, his historical greatness, and the universal applicability of his thought.

These contradictions are symptomatic of the effect of the bureaucracy in distorting and repressing broad areas of Chinese social life.

12. Science and Culture —Under Mao and Under Hua

The masses must be brutalized and demoralized if the minority rule of the bureaucracy is to be kept free from challenge. Debate must be quelled, not just on foreign and domestic political issues but on social, cultural, literary, and scientific questions. Every hole through which a private citizen might squeeze a criticism must be sealed off. (The exception that proves the rule in China is the permitting of factory shop-floor debate over the purely technical implementation of decisions already made higher up; these are characterized precisely by the fact that they never touch on any *general* question through which a discussion could begin of the political rule of the bureaucracy.)

Implicit in such a system is the need to make the only determinant of truth the will of the party leadership, subject to no external measure. Feudalist and capitalist ruling circles in their decline both sought similar means of stopping the historical clock—assuming that if no one could formulate the truth, no one could act on it. The Stalinists could well take for their motto the saying of Ignatius Loyola, who sought to save the temporal power of Catholicism in the sixteenth century: "We should always be disposed to believe that that which appears white is really black, if the hierarchy of the Church so decides."

This cultivation of a single monolithic standard, and a personal and arbitrary one at that, places Stalinism at odds not only with Marxism but with the conditions necessary for the development of any serious culture or even of modern science and industry.

This is rationalized through the syllogism that the party—ultimately, the self-perpetuating party hierarchy—in some mystical way embodies the will of the masses. Such delegation of powers is not subject to verification through discussion, debate, or vote, which is prevented by the bureaucracy. Correspondingly, scientific theory, materialism—all the great conquests of Marx and the early Marxists—must be completely eradicated. Critical reason must be devalued, so that there is no possible argument against the will of the monopolist bureaucracy that the party is bound to respect.

Such arbitrariness is inherent in the preservation of the Stalinist caste. It leads periodically to excesses that seem almost incomprehensible even from the standpoint of the enlightened self-interest of the bureaucracy. But there is method in the madness insofar as the substitution of the arbitrary will of the bureaucracy for the self-government of the working class is a precondition of the bureaucracy's continued existence.

Let us examine some features of the social life of China, to see the consequences of "socialism in one country" and the parasitic social formation that generates this theory.

*   *   *

Mao's semireligious cult of his own supposed godlike powers and his intolerance of rival ideas dealt heavy blows to culture, science, and technology. Instead of viewing these achievements of humanity as great treasures that had been unjustly monopolized by the capitalist ruling class, the Mao faction in his last years came to see all specialized learning or creation as inherently evil and dangerous.

In a speech on December 27, 1977, the head of the Chinese Academy of Sciences, Fang I, declared that since the Cultural Revolution began in 1966, "basic scientific and theoretical research in particular has been virtually done away with."[1] He said the previous government had "retarded the development of a whole generation of young people" in the study of science.[2]

The following January, Hsinhua ran an article under the provocative title, "Peking Library Lifts Ban on Chinese and Foreign Books." This said:

> During the past decade . . . the gang of four brushed aside all foreign works of literature as "feudal, bourgeois or revisionist poisonous weeds". They forbade publishing houses to put out such works and ordered the libraries to hold them back from circulation.[3]

The same treatment was accorded to almost all Chinese books written before 1966, with the exception of Mao's writings and technical works.

Since the death of Mao, Hua Kuo-feng has been trying to reestablish the credibility of his government by admitting a small part of what every Chinese knows about what things were like over the last decade.

The revelations began in general terms:

They [Chiang Ch'ing et al.] practised an unscrupulous sectarianism in literary and art circles, developed a coterie that ganged up to advance their own interests so that literary and art circles would become their "gang-dominated domain". . . . They trumped up charges against a great number of revolutionary literary and art workers and persecuted them and suppressed a great number of good or fairly good artistic works, including [the film] "Pioneers", which were created at great effort by artists trying to carry out Chairman Mao's revolutionary line in literature and art. . . .[4]

Such accusations are the stock in trade of the Maoist propaganda machine, and of the Kremlin's slander mills of Stalin's day. It is always difficult to guess what amount of truth, if any, lies beneath the vitriol. But the Chinese soon began to publish interviews with former political prisoners, mostly from the literary and art fields, who had been jailed without trial during and after the Cultural Revolution.

One dramatic account was that of Yuan Hsueh-fen, one of China's most famous actresses and singers in the 1950s and early 1960s. The new CCP leaders of Shanghai on their own initiative set up an interview between Yuan and the *Washington Post*.

Yuan was a member of the Communist Party, a three-time delegate to the National People's Congress, and a close personal friend of Premier Chou En-lai. She was a leading national star of the traditional Shaohsing Opera. In 1966, Mao and his faction branded traditional Chinese opera as bourgeois, which almost automatically made its performers suspected "capitalist-roaders" and "class enemies." Yuan Hsueh-fen was arrested and held for three years, then barred from the stage for another seven. The following is from her interview:

"They accused me of being a member of a certain KMT [Kuomintang] organization. . . .

"I was branded a bourgeois element, a rightist and a counterrevolutionary."

Yuan was put in a large mansion in the southern part of the city [Shanghai], locked by herself in one room. She estimates that at least 20 others were detained there in separate rooms, including professional storyteller Tang Ken-liang, who joined her in the interview.

A relative whom Yuan had asked to take care of her youngest child, born in 1966, was branded a landlord and the child had to be turned over to a maid. Her husband, a newspaper reporter, was forced to attend a work farm and then work as an editor in a publishing firm against his will.

She was not allowed to see her family for four years. While under detention, "I slept in my coat because I didn't know when I would be interrupted. They were always cursing me. They demanded that I write so-called confessions. I didn't count the number, but they probably held accusation meetings of me about 500 times. . . ."

In 1970, she was released but sent to a work farm and allowed to see her family only once or twice a month. . . .[5]

Yuan Hsueh-fen was a nationally known celebrity with personal connections in the highest level of China's leadership. She was not involved in politics per se, but was an artist. If these things could happen to her and no one could protest or even know, one can only imagine the situation of lesser artists who ran afoul of Mao's thought-control policy. What a baleful light such accounts shed on the realities of Mao's so-called Cultural Revolution. Nor was Yuan's ordeal over even when her captors themselves admitted they had no reason to hold her:

In 1973, she was cleared of all charges but not allowed to perform or to reveal her identity to the few voice and acting students she was allowed to tutor.

"I am an actress and I should practice the singing every day," she said, "but for 10 whole years I couldn't sing a single song of Shaohsing Opera."

The infallible leader and his infallible party do not make mistakes. . . .

This Kafkaesque system has not been dismantled. If it did not suit the factional purposes of the current leaders to permit Yuan Hsueh-fen to tell her story, she would not be allowed to do so.

In the *Guardian* article by Pat and Roger Howard mentioned earlier, these two loyal supporters of Hua Kuo-feng, living in Canton, give this report of the levels of repression under Mao in the period after the Cultural Revolution.

In units where factionalism was extremely serious the faction in power, convinced that they were the only representatives of the correct line, carried out fascist repression against those who had been labeled rightist and members of opposing factions. The methods included systematic public humiliation, kidnaping, torture and even murder. People in basic units were not the only victims of this form of fascism. For example, recent wall posters described what happened to Ho Lung. An old revolutionary fighter [Ho was a founder of the CCP's Red Army in 1927 and a member of its Central Committee for two decades], he was accused of being a rightist during the cultural revolution and put under detention. Only three fen (1½ cents) per day was allocated for his food and he was given only limited drinking water. It was under such circumstances that he died.

The most serious and far-reaching effect of the repression experienced or witnessed by the masses during the cultural revolution was to create a fear of criticizing the excesses that occurred and problems of real (and fake) ultra-"leftism." To do so might lay oneself open to being attacked as a rightist who was attempting to "reverse the correct verdicts" of the cultural revolution. Even in the vast majority of units which had not been directly affected, stories circulated about what happened to people labeled "rightist" in other units.[6]

In the late fall of 1977, American correspondent Harrison Salisbury visited China. While he was there, the new regime set up interviews for him with a large number of writers and artists. In his report on that visit he wrote:

It has been many years since foreign visitors have been able to meet with Chinese creative personalities. Five years ago, in two months of travel, the closest I was able to get to a writer was a brief discussion with Ho Chien, a nervous middle-aged woman who was literary editor of Wen Wei Bao [a Shanghai daily]. . . . She told me a bit about recent Chinese "literary achievements," the most significant of which seemed to have been publication of a story called "The Making of a Zipper," exhorting zipper makers to improve their product.

In 1977 the situation had swung around sharply. Not only did Chinese authorities find it possible to arrange meetings with cultural personalities but I also encountered some entirely by accident. The riddle of the nonpresence of writers and artists in 1972 was solved. Almost every person I met in 1977 had been in prison in 1972, or confined to his home, exiled to a farm in the countryside, or put to some other form of disgrace.

The accounts were much like that of Yuan Hsueh-fen. A few examples should suffice:

Liu Fuan. . . . is one of China's leading composers. When he heard the news [of the arrest of the "gang of four"], he did not smile; his feelings were too deep. Because during much of the past 10 years he had been confined to a narrow room, not permitted to see his family, not permitted to hear music, not permitted to compose.

Chou Chaio-yen is a small vibrant woman with a bittersweet smile and a good conversational knowledge of English. Before 1965 she was perhaps China's best-known soprano with a repertory of classical European songs. From the beginning of the Cultural Revolution until last autumn she was forbidden to sing. She was also forbidden to teach in the Shanghai Music Conservatory.

"Anything European," she said, "was considered 'worship of things foreign.' The only foreign composition which was permitted was the 'Internationale.'". . .

Chou Chaio was removed from her teaching post and compelled to work as a scrubwoman, cleaning floors and carrying water. Later she dug earth and laid bricks in air-raid shelters.[7]

The men who now rule China did make a timid attempt to steer their erratic helmsman back from the abyss in 1975. In that year Chou Yung-hsin became minister of education. His appointment was unusual in Mao's China, since he actually was a professional scientist and a member of the Academy of Sciences. According to one source: "He concluded, after investigation, that university standards in 1975 were no higher than those of technical middle schools before the Cultural Revolution."[8]

Chou Yung-hsin was denounced for trying to "whip up a professional typhoon" and for downgrading the importance of Mao Tsetung Thought. He died of a cerebral hemorrhage during a "struggle and criticism" session in which he was being publicly humiliated in the spring of 1976. The death was not reported by the Chinese press. (On August 28, 1977, Teng Hsiao-p'ing led a small ceremony for Chou Yung-hsin at Papaoshan Cemetery in Peking, posthumously reinstating him in the CCP.)[9]

While claiming that only the "gang of four" were responsible, Peking today is repeating Chou Yung-hsin's charges in even stronger terms. Fox Butterfield gave this report in the *New York Times*:

Chinese educators are . . . now admitting that over the past 10 years, since the start of the Cultural Revolution, the school system has hindered the development of a highly trained modern labor force that China needed.

An official at the Higher Education Bureau of the Ministry of Education in Peking told another visiting American scholar, Suzanne Pepper, that the mistakes of the past decade had "spoiled two generations."[10]

The most bitter comments, however, are not relayed through the *New York Times* but appear directly in the Chinese government-controlled press. The Peking *Kwangming Daily* published an article entitled "All-Round Implementation of the Party's Policy Towards Intellectuals." A Hsinhua summary of the article said in part:

The gang of four declared: "We prefer workers without culture to exploiters with culture and intellectual aristocrats." They condemned intellectuals as "exploiters and intellectual aristocrats" who did nothing but eat under socialism, "maggots" that "undermine the socialist economic base".

Chang Chun-chiao said such nonsense that "it would be better for the intellectuals to forget everything they had learned from primary school to college." Yao Wen-yuan clamoured that the Chinese intellectuals had "the sham academic knowledge of the bourgeoisie". They spread the lie "Once one acquires knowledge one becomes bourgeois" and "One who acquires professional competency forgets the dictatorship of the proletariat".

In the areas and departments under their control [in fact, the whole government—L.E.], the gang of four slashed a large number of institutions of scientific research, culture and education and attempted to dispense with various types of specialized personnel. Some major enterprises sent more than two thirds of their technical personnel to work for years on farms, so that it was impossible for them to do their own jobs.*[11]

All of these things were justified during Mao's lifetime through nebulous allusions to "class struggle," the need to guard against the threat of capitalist restoration, the danger that bourgeois ideas in the abstract, severed from an actual class of capitalist proprietors, were preparing the ground for active counterrevolution. At every slackening of the party's hold on the masses, the Maoists would grab hold of these ideological skeletons and rattle the bones in people's faces, after the manner of priests invoking the terror of hellfire and damnation to bring an unruly congregation back to the revealed orthodoxy. (It is not coincidental that the lexicon of Maoism is filled with words taken over from the vocabulary of superstition: ghosts, freaks, demons, etc.)

There is no point in engaging in a scholastic debate with the Maoists over what level of creative potential of the masses could and should be unlocked by a genuine workers' government in a society of the future. But at the least we can contrast the stultifying backwater engendered by Mao to the achievements in

---

*We might compare Mao's attitude toward scientists and technicians to Lenin's. Back in 1921, when Lenin was dealing almost exclusively with scientists trained under the tsarist regime, he wrote: "The Communist who has failed to prove his ability to bring together and guide the work of specialists in a spirit of modesty, going to the heart of the matter and studying it in detail, is a potential menace. We have many such Communists among us, and I would gladly swap dozens of them for one conscientious qualified bourgeois specialist" ("Integrated Economic Plan" [February 21, 1921], *Collected Works*, vol. 32, p. 144).

culture and education by a country such as Cuba, the only workers' state without a Stalinist bureaucracy. Cuba, with its nine and a half million people, has barely a hundredth of China's enormous population. The threat of foreign intervention and counterrevolution is far more immediate for Cuba than for China, existing as it does on the very doorstep of American imperialism. Yet the range of Cuba's cultural and artistic production in the years since the revolution puts China to shame, despite important bureaucratic abuses such as the arrest and trial of the poet Heberto Padilla in 1971.

The Ballet Nacional de Cuba, headed by world famous ballerina Alicia Alonso, is among the finest in the world and has been heavily supported by the Castro government since 1959. It has been singularly free of government constraints in its material— its critically acclaimed opening in New York in June 1978 featured everything from nineteenth-century classics to settings of Garcia Lorca tragedies, and a series of abstract and allegorical pieces newly created within the company. Cuban films have dealt intelligently and wittily with a wide range of social and political themes and produced a number of innovative directors who have won an international audience for their productions.

In education, too, Cuba has set a different priority and shown a different possibility than Mao's China. Today, with 130,000 students at the university level, tiny Cuba has more than a quarter of the entire number of college students China has. One of the slogans of the Mao period was to open the universities to students of worker or peasant class origin. But drastically reducing the numbers who could enroll meant that the great majority of workers and peasants could have no hope of a college education for themselves or their children. To really open the colleges to the oppressed means first of all expanding them. Under Mao, one Chinese out of every 1,800 was able to go to college; in Cuba the figure is one out of every 73.

The record of the Mao period is plain enough. The improvements in the two years since Mao's death, however, remain sparse. The "modernizers" around Hua recognize, at least, that it is not possible to dispense with modern science. In March 1977, the Academy of Science held a forum in Peking on the subject "letting one hundred schools of thought contend." One speaker, foreign-trained physicist Yen Chi-tzu, said that scientists "must apply themselves to their special fields of study if they are to make any contributions at all. What's wrong to be a specialist?

We should strive to be specialists, or better still authorities. . . ."[12]

This speech would have been heresy in Mao's day. It is a measure of the primitiveness of Maoist politics that it took a palace revolt to make such a speech possible, and that the public statement of such an elementary proposition as Yen's should seem like a great step forward.

Many of Mao's educational "reforms" have been quietly junked. Examinations have been reinstituted, requirements for part-time manual labor by students have been sharply curtailed, and science students, at least, are now permitted to go directly from high school to college instead of spending two or more years on work farms in the countryside. The massive program of shipping millions of "educated youth"—actually high school and junior high school graduates—to the countryside for two-year-to-life indefinite stays seems to be grinding to a halt. Since Mao's death, young people are now mainly sent to communes on the outskirts of their home cities.

China's new leaders are reestablishing a real university system, to replace the seminaries run by Mao. But the outlook for cultural and artistic freedom is more bleak. For all the diatribes against the sectarianism and repressive actions of the "gang of four," creativity under Hua thus far remains below even what is permitted under the Stalinist governments of the Soviet Union and Eastern Europe.

The signal for the limits of liberalization came almost immediately after the arrest of Chiang Ch'ing. The CCP has a well-worn formula, familiar to every literate Chinese, for explaining its current line. Articles in the Chinese press are of two kinds: abstract statements of line, and model examples of how the line is to be carried out. No one in China is foolish enough to act on line articles, if they are comprehensible at all, before seeing the models that define what the line really means.

On the art and literature front, for example:

We must fight to usher in the bright springtime in which a hundred flowers of socialist literature and art blossom together. . . .[13]

That sounds pretty good. Maoists around the world will quote that sentence to show that working people in China are now free to become artists, and that artists are free to use their talents creatively. The Chinese artist must watch more closely, for the approved examples of what the government considers to be flowers. The new model was provided in an article entitled "Northwest China Peasant Painters Hail Great Victory." This was an account of paintings on display at Sian. These included murals with titles such as "Down With the Wang-Chang-Chiang-Yao Anti-Party Clique" and "The Ferreting Out of the 'Gang of Four' Is Much to the Satisfaction of the People."[14]

In the spring of 1977 the Peking Art Gallery sponsored a National Art Exhibition, where more of the newly grown flowers were put on display. No abstract art here. Nor did any of the landscapes for which Chinese artists are so justly famous make it into the running at the National Art Exhibition. Here is how *China Reconstructs* conducts the tour:

> In the first hall of the exhibition was a huge oil painting, *With You in Charge, I Am at Ease,* depicting Chairman Mao and Chairman Hua discussing the affairs of the country. Comrade Hua is holding a sheet of paper Chairman Mao has given him on which he has written, **"With you in charge, I am at ease".** The artist has expressed love for Chairman Mao and trust in Chairman Hua.[15]

The accompanying full-page color photograph shows a benign Mao Tsetung, painted in soft focus with baby skin and a cherubic smile, patting Hua on the hand. Both men look twenty years younger than their actual ages. Hua leans forward attentively, his overly red cheeks glistening. He wears the symbols of bureaucratic authority. They are not gaudy, like the robes of Vatican churchmen or the rows of medals sported by Soviet generals. But their meaning is not lost on ordinary citizens: the hand-tailored Mao jacket, the fountain pen in the breast pocket, and the real leather shoes, which in the painting gleam as though they were made of glass.

How does this repellent egotism square with the CCP's constant drive to snuff out individualism, to eliminate self-interest, to compel working people to subordinate themselves to the dictates of the party without question or reservation? The truth is that the Chinese Stalinists are not against selfishness and egotism at all: they are just against anyone counterposing their personal needs or the interests of the peasant and working classes to the claims of the bureaucratic hierarchy.

The culture of this uncontrolled bureaucracy reflects its true nature more accurately than perhaps any other aspect of Chinese life. Art in China today is not a creative act of exploration, sharpening human perceptions and training the sense of beauty. The bureaucracy sees beauty only in its own mawkishly romanticized self-image. The narcissism and tasteless vanity that dominate this art would be seen as a mental aberration if it was exhibited by a private individual. But when a powerful head of state has his portrait painted in such a style, then displays the painting in an art gallery he controls, appoints judges who find it an excellent specimen of the creativity of the masses, and then has millions of reproductions printed and distributed around the world, that is supposed to be socialist art. The bureaucracy's notion of beauty is an embalmed likeness of its masters. These same masters imagine that every Chinese would find his or her life enhanced if they could have copies of these morticians' daubings on the wall of their home.

The right to read in Mao's China was as circumscribed as the right to paint. There have been some changes here as well. A Shanghai correspondent of the *Far Eastern Economic Review* gave one report on the post-Mao situation at that city's Fudan University in the spring of 1977:

> An early development occurred in January when the notice-board of the department of Chinese literature carried an article by students requesting a widening in scope of the literature course. . . .
> Since then, many posters have appeared, either criticising members of the university hierarchy for being in league with the gang of four, or praising those who received harsh treatment for opposing the four. . . .
> The first effect of these developments on the academic lives of the students is that the literature course has become wider in scope. When the university still suffered under the cultural dominance of Chiang Ching and her three disgraced colleagues, teachers were not even permitted to mention the names of authors criticised before or during the Cultural Revolution. As a result, it is possible that some students were unaware of such literary figures as Lao She and Pa Chin, not to mention authors of less international standing.
> . . . Students who knew of these authors assumed that their names were not mentioned because they had been dead for many years. In fact, Pa Chin still lives in Shanghai today.[16]

In comparison to the literary porridge of the last decade, when the books were burned and the libraries sealed, 1977 provided a veritable feast for hungry readers. At the end of the year the government announced the publication for the first time since the Cultural Revolution of collections of classical Chinese poetry, of a number of prerevolutionary novels by Communist authors, of several books by post-1949 Chinese novelists, and even the reissuing of Shakespeare, Victor Hugo, Tolstoy, Goethe, Cervantes, and Dante, as well as the philosophical writings of Hegel. That these works could have been extirpated from the culture of a quarter of the human race in the name of advancing socialism is testimony itself to the affinity between the cult of Mao Tsetung Thought and religious defenders of established power, who well know the value of an ignorant populace as a bulwark of their rule.

The thirst for knowledge, for the right to read something better than the dreary propaganda of the party machine, is indicated by a report that a line a hundred yards long formed at a Peking bookstore to buy the first copies of *Hamlet* to go on sale in China in more than a decade.[17]

For the first year and a half the Hua regime pretty much limited the revival of foreign authors to eighteenth- and nineteenth-century figures, or even earlier classics. But in March of 1978 it took a plunge into the twentieth century with the publication of a three-volume collection of Einstein's works, including a volume of his philosophical writings and a volume of his social and political essays. The reviews of this collection in the Chinese press marked a noticeable change of tone from the Mao days:

It goes without saying that Einstein was not free of the faults and limitations of his time. The seeking of truth and serving the interests of humanity, however, remained a goal throughout his life. The spiritual fruits of his labour and his strenuous defiance of violence can never be eclipsed. He is a giant shining star in the history of mankind.[18]

Two years before, the word *humanity* appeared in Maoist literature only as the target of polemics explaining how it dulled proletarian combativity by leaving out the class divisions in society. And certainly, at that time, China's sky was not large enough to hold two giant shining stars.

These changes by the new regime are welcome. They eliminate one of the more bizarre sides of Maoism. Thus far, however, the thaw has not proceeded as far as the temporary relaxation of the censors under Khrushchev in the Soviet Union in the late 1950s— which saw the legal publication of Solzhenitsyn's *One Day in the Life of Ivan Denisovitch,* that searing account of life in Stalin's labor camps. Nor has it gone so far even as the critical and satirical literature permitted today in such bureaucratized workers' states as Hungary, Poland, and Yugoslavia. Still, the improvement is real, reflecting an important concession to mass pressure for the right to read. As such it is part of a dynamic process that has not yet run its course.

13. Justice, Repression, and Political Prisoners

One prevalent theme of the fellow-traveling Western literature about China under Mao is the supposed absence of repression and the spirit of unfeigned solidarity that pervades all of Chinese social life. John Gurley asserts:

> . . . the Chinese are striving not only for a high level of efficiency but also for human relationships within the work process that are in harmony with their revolutionary goals of eliminating social divisions of labor, promoting enthusiasm for work based on collective and moral incentives, reducing the hierarchical structures that subordinate workers and peasants to "bosses" and humble them before experts and technicians, encouraging self-sufficiency at all levels, and fashioning working and living environments that are nonalienating, warm, and cooperative, and in general worthy of human beings.[1]

On the face of it, these claims are contradicted by the very existence of the bureaucratic caste, by the antidemocratic and thoroughly alienating methods used in the purges and in setting national policy. Moreover, there are many ways in which a regime may be repressive, not all of which are as gross as the mass executions of Stalin's Russia. The parasitic bureaucracy maintains its hold on the Chinese workers' state through the exercise of totalitarian control not only over the overt acts of groups in Chinese society but down even to the level of individual thought.

The first step in this process is to seal off the population from contact with the outside world. The rationalization for this is to prevent the undermining of "socialism" by imperialist spies. The effect is the most complete negation of internationalism. Is international socialism conceivable when no one but government functionaries is permitted to leave the country and the few foreigners let in are treated with officially organized suspicion and walled off from contact with ordinary people?

Simon Leys, who lived in Maoist China for extended periods, describes the limitations placed by the government on any real mingling between Chinese and foreigners—and the restricted field of vision permitted to visitors:

China has hundreds of cities, only about a dozen are open to ordinary foreigners. In each one, the foreigners are always put in the same hotel—usually a huge palace, set like a fortress in the middle of a vast garden, far away in a distant suburb. . . .

Out of the tens of thousands of villages where more than 80 percent of the Chinese people live, foreigners visit less than a dozen (and always the same ones). . . .

The same treatment has been given to the Chinese population: out of eight hundred million Chinese, foreigners meet about sixty individuals. The literary world is represented by two or three writers, always the same, who take care of visiting men of letters; the same is true of scientists, scholars, and so on.[2]

The effects of this forced isolation are far-reaching.* The first is that no information about the outside world is directly available to the Chinese people. They may not as individuals subscribe to foreign periodicals, their mail is effectively censored, they meet no one from a different culture. This moves in a direction diametrically opposed to that of Marxism and socialist internationalism.

In addition to keeping the rest of the world out, these arrangements keep the Chinese people in. Passports for foreign travel are rarely issued except on government business. This is a violation of an elementary human right. But it does not end there. Maoist China has followed the example of Stalin's Russia in imposing a

---

*Mao did not invent this practice but revived it. The compulsory isolation of China's people from foreign influences was a reactionary tradition of imperial days. Robert S. Elegant describes the impression this custom made on Matteo Ricci, the Jesuit missionary, when he first went to China at the end of the sixteenth century:

"Accustomed to the freedom of Europe, Ricci was shocked by the discovery that unofficial travelers from neighboring lands were never permitted to leave China and that *no* foreigner might travel freely within the country for fear that he might later tell unsuitable tales abroad" (*The Center of the World: Communism and the Mind of China* [New York: Funk and Wagnalls, 1968], p. 30).

It should be noted that Leys is writing of the Mao years, and that the restrictions seem to have been slightly loosened since Mao's death, though the basic picture remains accurate.

system of internal passports that effectively prevent an individual from quitting a job, moving to another city, and often, even from taking a brief trip. (After Stalin's death, this system was abolished in the Soviet Union, a fact occasionally cited by hardcore Maoists, such as Martin Nicolaus, as proof that capitalism has been restored there. The USSR still places severe restrictions on the right of Soviet citizens to leave the country.)

These travel restrictions have long been a source of complaint against the bureaucracy. In the Hundred Flowers Bloom campaign in the spring of 1957 when the Chinese press was—for a few weeks—opened to critical letters to the editor, many of the protests focused on this question. One example was a May 17, 1957, letter to Mao from Yang Shih-chan, a professor of accountancy at the Central-South Institute of Finance and Economics. Yang wrote:

> Our Constitution provides that citizens "enjoy freedom of residence and freedom to change residence." In fact, we have not given any of the 500 million peasants the freedom to change their residence to a city. . . .
>
> This is tyranny![3]

This aspect of Chinese life has not changed in the years since. Australian China scholar Ross Terrill, on a visit to a chemical-fiber plant near Nanking in 1971, asked the spokesman of the factory's Revolutionary Committee: "Can a worker transfer work by his own individual decision?" The reply: *"I-ting pu-shih!"* ("Certainly not!").[4]

A more detailed account was provided by Canadian journalist Ross Munro, stationed for two years in Peking:

> People are normally assigned to a work unit for life. Transfers are extremely difficult to obtain, but are sometimes granted on the condition that the departing worker find someone with comparable skills and experience who is willing to switch jobs with him. On lamp posts in Peking, one sometimes sees poignant little notices asking if any worker here might consider switching jobs with someone working in a distant town. The writer of the notice sometimes appeals for sympathy, declaring that he wants to rejoin his family in Peking which he has seen only two weeks a year for the past decade.[5]

In a later article Munro described the elaborate system of travel documents and ration coupons that restrict movement for working people in China:

> Even a short trip away from one's village or city is difficult to arrange

despite the official assertion, technically correct, that Chinese citizens are free to travel. . . .

The would-be traveller first goes to the leader of his unit—a factory workshop, a production team in a commune or whatever other organization he works for—and asks for leave from work and permission to travel. He has to come up with a concrete reason for needing leave—such as a sick parent in another city—because the only vacation time regularly granted in China amounts to five or six days of national holidays each year. The only regular exception to this rule applies to the large number of married couples who live apart; then the husband usually gets one or two weeks a year to visit his wife and family.

Once he gets permission from his work unit, the would-be traveller must then obtain special ration coupons which allow him to buy rice or bread outside his province.

A system of local and national ration coupons is one of the most basic of the control mechanisms used in China. Ordinarily, families are issued grain coupons which are valid only in their home province. They cannot buy as much as a bowl of rice in a restaurant in another province unless they present the much-prized national coupons which are issued only to high-ranking officials and to people whose travel plans have been approved by their work units.[6]

Munro's account does not differ either in essentials or in details from many similar reports. The one point in it that might seem surprising is the compulsory separation of husbands and wives by assigning them to work in different cities. This has been confirmed to this author by several Chinese friends who have told of being asked by relatives in China to write letters to the government appealing that they be reunited with their spouses. The only thing that might be added to his account is that such involuntary separations are far more likely if the people involved are under political suspicion.

Beyond this web of restraints and restrictions lie the units themselves, where virtually all Chinese carry on their lives and work. Are these then the "nonalienating, warm, and cooperative" enclaves within an otherwise totally repressed society? Let us once again seek the testimony of ordinary Chinese citizens during that brief moment in 1957 when such things were published. A letter to the Peking *Daily Worker* signed by ten members of the Shanghai Trade Union Council on the internal life of China's trade unions in its major industrial city reads, in part:

Once a managing director or Party committee has made a decision, nothing can be done but to leave it as it is even though it is clearly unreasonable. And trade union cadres, even if they do not agree with it, can do nothing but try to persuade the masses to act accordingly. Even if they are called names and scolded, they can only keep silent and show a smiling face; otherwise, they will be accused of "fomenting discord" and "not being determined to carry out the will of the leadership." As to mass supervision, it is out of the question for the trade unions. Even today, when Chairman Mao's report on correct handling of internal contradictions has been widely relayed, if trade unions publish criticisms put forward by the workers against the leadership and present the widespread views of the masses to the management and the Party committees, they are questioned like this: "You are mobilising the masses to open a 'struggle' meeting and criticise the leadership, aren't you? . . ."[7]

And twenty years later? One valuable piece of testimony comes from the authors of *Deuxième Retour de Chine*, published recently in France. Claudie and Jacques Broyelle and Evelyne Tschirhart are not Sinologues or reporters for the Western capitalist press. All three were Maoists who lived in China for two years as employees of the Chinese government, returning to France in January 1975. All three had visited China previously, in the late 1960s or early 1970s.

They found their extended stay and close exposure to Maoism on its home ground a disillusioning experience. They were able to witness at firsthand elements of Chinese life that are closed to ordinary foreign visitors. In particular, they were able to attend some of the workers' discussion meetings that are so famous in the literature of Maoism. Here is their description of what actually takes place at these affairs as they witnessed them:

Since the leadership sets the agenda, as well as introducing and closing the discussion, the workers cannot permit themselves to react any more freely than they would in general toward the leadership. The meeting is characterized by a sing-song, liturgical psalmody of the party's slogans of the moment. If one uses here the word "discussion," it is for want of a better term. No one "discusses" in the proper sense of the word. If several people in turn undertake to speak, they take infinite precautions to avoid responding to something someone else might have said, purely inadvertently, that could be interpreted as having anything to do with reality or with raising a problem. There is, then, a sort of round table. Here, if each person speaks essentially on the same subject, this is not because this subject is to be discussed in common, but because on this particular day it serves as a pretext to reaffirm that everything is going well; that, nevertheless, the class struggle continues; that, while only 70 percent is positive and there still exist old reactionary ideas in the heads of some people, nevertheless the main current is revolution; that it is necessary to study well, work well, to persevere in combatting bad thoughts; and above all, to strengthen the sole leadership of the party.[8]

The regime does not rely entirely on social pressure to maintain this mummified atmosphere. The Broyelles and Evelyne Tschirhart describe the consequences for failure to conform to the script:

> The obligatory political meeting unfolds in the presence of a leader. One would have to be crazy to raise criticisms that go beyond the accepted limits. But one would have to be equally crazy to hold one's tongue, since, as [Edgar] Snow notes, "the right to remain silent does not exist." One would thereby risk a few trifling inconveniences, ranging from not being able to obtain housing or a place at the day care center, up to the loss of one's civic rights and voluntary transfer to the countryside.[9]

The consequences of such a system on social relationships can be imagined. Simon Leys cites one common response in a series of interviews with acquaintances in Hong Kong in 1975 who were recent refugees from China:

> M— —, who is a teacher from Kwangchow, tells me that one never discusses politics with people one does not know well, or even with close friends if those friends belong to one's political unit; one speaks of political matters only with close friends who belong to other units. The reason: within the same unit, people always risk having mutually to accuse each other. Everyone prefers, therefore, not only to reveal as little as possible about himself to potential accusers but, above all, to know as little as possible about friends whom sooner or later he may be led to denounce. Ignorance makes it possible at least in good faith to confine these obligatory denunciations to a routine formality.[10]

Deuxième Retour de Chine refers to certain punishments that lie in wait for a worker or student who deviates from the confessional ritual of the mandatory "discussion" meetings. But who decides such things? How can they be appealed? What rights do Chinese citizens have that the government is bound to respect?

The most elementary limitation that must be placed on a hierarchical structure before we can speak of workers' democracy, or even of bourgeois democracy, is that administrators be stripped of the right to arbitrarily arrest and imprison people they do not like. This has become a major focus of the dissident movement in the Soviet Union under the slogan of the fight for Soviet legality. This demand has been fought for by the working class in every capitalist country for a hundred years and more.

Leaving aside for a moment the very elastic definition of what constitutes a crime in the eyes of the bureaucracy, Chinese Stalinist jurisprudence operates on the principle that the accused is guilty until proven innocent. The consequence of this stance is that anyone accused by the authorities of a political or social breach of conduct is held in jail until brought to trial. There is no bail. Preventive detention is the officially approved policy. This was debated briefly back in the days of the Hundred Flowers, and the party hierarchy replied to its critics among the masses that to presume someone innocent until proven guilty or to allow them to remain at liberty until they had been convicted was to protect the guilty from punishment and to place the interests of the guilty above those of the people. The "people" were not allowed to say anything on this subject.

The authors of *Deuxième Retour* add to this picture: "To our knowledge there is no maximum limit to the length of preventive detention."[11]

They give one example from among their own acquaintances in Peking, in the community of foreign Maoists who work for the bureaucracy. A number of these, who had lived in China for many years and were nicknamed the "old foreigners," were arbitrarily arrested by the Mao faction during the Cultural Revolution.

Among the "old foreigners" arrested since the end of 1967, some remained in prison more than five years without, in the end, being brought to trial or even, for the most part, being accused of any specific crime. One fine day in 1973 they were simply released. Certain Chinese still regard them as basically guilty, if of nothing else, at least of having been in prison. They themselves often took a long time after their release to realize that they were innocent.[12]

The Broyelles and Evelyne Tschirhart had the opportunity to speak to released prisoners and learn from them the conditions under which they had been held (remember that these were people who had not been convicted of anything):

Throughout the time he is imprisoned, the accused person vanishes completely into the innards of Security. He may receive neither letters nor visits; he may not send letters to the outside, or even, frequently, keep a journal. His only reading matter consists of *Renmin Ribao* [*People's Daily*] and Marxist classics. His family will not know for a long time whether he is dead or alive. The accused person's spouse will lose his or her job; their children will be expelled from school. The prisoner knows all this, and it may be assumed that, with this in mind, he will channel his confessions into the desired mold.

Still worse, perhaps, than secret confinement, is the refusal to inform the accused person of the charges against him. He will simply be made aware that he has done wrong, leaving it up to him to confess particular crimes, i.e., to make a self-indictment. He is presumed guilty, and furthermore, no trouble is taken to furnish proof of his guilt. He is the one who must provide it. While confessions are not extracted by torture—that, at least, is what Mao wants—although total isolation may be called a form of torture; they are nevertheless one of the props of the whole system.[13]

Eventually the prisoner may come to trial. Most of these procedures are closed to the public. Some are held before "mass tribunals," in which a crowd is assembled to hear a prisoner's confession and condemn him or her. In either case the prisoner is at a distinct disadvantage. What is a crime? What is a legitimate sentence? Back in 1951 a law was issued on the repression of counterrevolutionaries. Article 10 of this law specified as a criminal "anyone who attempts to sow discord between the various national minorities, the democratic classes, the various democratic and popular groups, or who attempts to weaken the bonds that unite the population with the government. . . . as well as anyone who engages in counterrevolutionary propaganda, or invents or repeats false rumors."[14]

Such a law can be interpreted to prohibit any criticism whatsoever of the regime or its representatives. The penalty for conviction was a minimum of three years in prison and a maximum of death.

In the first decade of Maoist rule the laws were at least written down, however vague they might be. There were even practicing lawyers who could defend in court those people who did not understand the intricacies of the law code. In the Cultural Revolution the profession of lawyer was abolished on the ground that the people of China had been so politically educated that they understood the law and everyone was capable of defending themselves before a judge. But in 1957 the old law code was withdrawn and no new one has ever been issued. It is reported that judges have a private set of laws that they are able to consult, but ordinary people know the law only by word of mouth and rumor.

To Western radicals, acquainted with a capitalist legal system in which the law is used to cheat and oppress the masses, it might seem that written laws are intrinsically restrictive, generally designed to uphold private property, and probably best eliminated. However, through struggle the masses have been able to get certain democratic rights written into law. And even the most repressive legal code contains within it an implicit bill of rights, through the assumption that one cannot be punished for doing something that the law does not say is a crime. That is why the most authoritarian regimes prefer to rule without a written law code. This is not a Marxist innovation on Mao's part but the revival of the legal system—or lack of one—of the old Chinese emperors, whose absolute and arbitrary power was not subordinate to any law.

The Marxist tradition in this realm is just the opposite of what Mao has done. It is founded on extending and protecting the rights of the working class and the rest of the masses, not the arbitrary expansion of the power of the state administration. Justice must be uniform and objective. In the young Soviet Union the leadership worked to establish a common national law code as an essential part of the fight for social justice and for culture. Lenin's writings on this question sharply attack the reactionary idea of even regional standards of written law, much less individual standards of unwritten law. In May 1922 he wrote:

Failure to make allowances for local differences in all these matters would mean slipping into bureaucratic centralism, and so forth. . . . Nevertheless, the law must be uniform, and the root evil of our social life, and of our lack of culture, is our pandering to the ancient Russian view and semi-savage habit of mind, which wishes to preserve Kaluga law as distinct from Kazan law. . . . Unless we strictly adhere to this most elementary condition for maintaining the uniformity of the law for the whole Federation, it will be utterly impossible to protect the law, or to develop any kind of culture.[15]

In place of this kind of uniform written national code, the Maoists use the courts, or less formal bodies in local units, simply as the enforcement arm of the party, in which nothing is written down and appeal is well-nigh impossible.

Occasionally, in nonpolitical cases, friends of the accused have used wall posters to try to win reconsideration of particularly harsh or unjust sentences. Ross Munro describes an example of this:

In the summer of 1973, a young man named Chang accompanied his girl friend to an out-of-the-way place in their factory where they proceeded to make love. Unfortunately, some fellow workers happened upon them in the middle of their love-making.

The couple's activity not being publicly acceptable behavior, . . . the leadership of the Sian Western Electrical Factory, where they worked, proceeded to take disciplinary action. The factory first decided that this was an internal matter, which shouldn't be taken to the outside authorities. Instead, the two young people would be subjected to criticism for their "bourgeois lifestyle."

Unfortunately for young Chang, his girl friend's father was an important official who came to Sian when he heard the news. Once there, he succeeded in pressuring his dishonored daughter into changing her story and charging her boy friend with rape.

So the outside authorities took charge of the case and Chang appeared in court. Chang apparently wasn't too happy with this turn of events because the court officials declared that he had a "bad attitude" toward his crime. This bad attitude, the court declared, justified a 20-year sentence.

The court itself raised serious questions about the entire affair by sentencing the victim of the rape to three years of education-through-labor in some sort of detention centre. She was convicted of having a bad lifestyle.

Many of Chang's work-mates were so appalled by what had happened that they took advantage of the fluid political situation in 1975 and 1976 to put up wall posters in Sian describing the incident and decrying the fate of their friend.[16]

The ultimate destination of those who fall into the hands of the security system is usually not prison but a rural labor camp. Prisons, such as the "model" Prison Number One in Peking—one of the few that foreigners ever see—are little more than temporary holding places for prisoners destined for the camps.

Incidentally, one does not have to be considered a criminal to wind up in the camps. *Deuxième Retour* explains this novel idea:

Since August 1, 1957, a decision of the State Council, which on August 4 of that same year became the law "for the transformation of the idle," authorized the sending to reeducation through labor farms of vagrants, young delinquents, persons fired from their jobs, those who refuse to accept labor discipline or who disobey orders, or even those who "do not show enthusiasm in productive work, who seek quarrels without reason, who obstruct public services, and who do not correct themselves despite efforts to educate them."[17]

The police are not the only ones who can put somebody away in this manner. It is a purely administrative decision that can be made by any work unit, school administration, or neighborhood Revolutionary Committee, requiring only the approval of local authorities. No tribunal or hearing is involved.

The most extensive account of the camps comes from Bao Ruo-wang, also known as Jean Pasqualini. Bao, the son of a Corsican father and a Chinese mother, grew up in China. He spent seven years in the labor camps. He was released in 1964 as a gesture to France when France recognized the People's Republic. He has described what he lived through in his book, *Prisoner of Mao.* Mao Tsetung learned much from Stalin. He never tired of acknowledging this debt, despite his occasional criticism of his mentor. When the Chinese camps were established, the Soviet model was stressed. Then-Minister of Security Lo Jui-ch'ing, in a report on September 7, 1954, said:

> The preparation of a draft law concerning reform through labor in the People's Republic of China began some time ago. During its preparation, the authors have obtained the collaboration of Soviet jurists and this project has been the subject of numerous discussions and modifications. We consider preventive detention to be one of the mechanisms of reform through labor. This corresponds entirely to the spirit of the democratic legislative system of the people. The decisions of the Soviet Code on reform through labor are the same.[18]

One of the things the CCP's secret police learned from Soviet jurists was that particularly monstrous innovation of the Soviet labor camp: setting the food ration of prisoners on a piecework basis, tied to their production quota. One is faced thereby with the choice of working at a normal pace and starving, or working to the physical limit of endurance to get enough to eat. Bau Ruo-wang describes how this worked in 1958 in his first year of prison (it did not change in the period of his incarceration). He was assigned to be a folder, folding by hand the pages of newly printed, unbound books.

A prisoner's food depended on his production. My portions as a beginner would be low, and I had two weeks to reach a level of output that would either maintain it at that level, raise it to first class—or drop it down to a punishment level. But beyond production, [my cellmate] warned me (and I could have guessed anyway), a prisoner's attitude was equally important for determining rations. Even a good folder could fall down to subsistence rations if he worked without evident enthusiasm, or if he sloughed off in study sessions.

Rations were divided into four categories: beginner, light labor, heavy and punishment. The rate for beginners—those who could not fold a minimum of 3,000 leaves—was calculated at 14 kilos, 250 grams of cereal per month—about 31 pounds in all. [This comes to about 1,600 calories a day.—L.E.] This might not seem too bad, were it not for the fact that our diet contained almost no fat, therefore obliging our bodies to seek their force from starch alone. Meat was almost unknown—except on festive occasions—and it was only rarely that the cooks found a little grease to add to the corn mush or vegetable soup. . . . The prisoners always watched each other's rations like hawks, wary lest someone else receive a few grams more.

What created harsh animosities was the mixing of different levels of rations in the same cell—a common occurrence, and one that a good cell leader tried by all means to eliminate.[19]

For much of the time Bao was in the camps, the workday required to maintain normal food rations was set at about sixteen hours.

Bao touches on one other aspect of this system of repression. That is the difficulty of ever getting out of the camps once one is inside, whatever the original reason. He describes a discussion on this question he had with a fellow prisoner in the early 1960s. This prisoner had been a judge before his arrest and knew how sentences were arrived at. Bao writes:

> First, he said, there is nothing in China to limit the sentencing power of the government. The common analogy is the rubber band—a sentence can be stretched or abbreviated, depending on dozens of nonobjective factors. A man sentenced to life might well become a free worker before his cellmate who was sentenced to ten years. . . . If, as in my case, the actual sentence was twelve years, they might announce twenty to him [the prisoner], or even life. As always, the prisoner is told that he can lighten his sentence by making the necessary efforts and showing himself to be a model for the others. So perhaps after one year of furious effort he will be rewarded by a gift from the state: a sentence reduction from life to twenty years. Radiant and grateful, he becomes even more so the perfect prisoner, and after three more years he is reduced to only fifteen years. Two years later the sentence is reduced to ten years—ten more years only! Since he has already served five, and continues to behave with zeal and gratitude, they wait until he has served seven more (to make his original twelve years). It is at this moment that the government, in its generosity, decides on an amnesty. Twelve years instead of life! The man becomes a free worker with a song in his heart, thinking only of helping to build socialism.[20]

One can hardly blame Bao for his cynicism. Such heartbreaking cat-and-mouse moral torture is debasing, to its executors as much as to its victims. That it is carried out in the name of socialism does more damage to the cause of human emancipation than anything the open and avowed enemies of the working class could have done. It is a hundred times less damaging to the morale of the proletariat to suffer a defeat in open battle than it is to be betrayed by its own leaders, cut to ribbons, and sold into bondage.

This counterrevolutionary role of Stalinism, including its

Chinese variant, is revealed in its choice of victims. Into its prison camps and horror chambers goes every worker who dares to stand up for the rights of their class, every genuine revolutionist who challenges the reactionary rule of the petty-bourgeois caste.

Among the first targets of the Mao government on the Left were the Chinese Trotskyists. They were supporters of the revolution of 1949, long-time participants in the Chinese labor movement who had suffered persecution under the Kuomintang. Their crime was that they spoke among the masses in favor of making a reality out of the many socialist and democratic promises made by the CCP in its first years in power. The CCP's reply was not to prove before the masses that it meant what it said, but to order the arrest of its working class critics. At the end of December 1952 and the beginning of January 1953, some three hundred Chinese Trotskyists were arrested. Five of them, whose ultimate fate is unknown, managed to write an appeal to the world working class on January 28, 1953, and have it smuggled out of China. They wrote:

We five, the signatories of this document, are up to the present the only ones lucky enough to have escaped the recent wholesale arrests of Trotskyists. In the past we were in the forefront of the struggle to overthrow the Kuomintang regime, and today we still stand firmly at our posts in the effort for national construction. We are all communists. . . .

[In the fall of 1949] the CP mobilized an anti-Trotskyist campaign in two districts, Wenchow of Chekiang Province and Shunsan of Kwangtung Province . . . and arrested many of them. Some were shot on the false charge of being "Kuomintang agents."

When they were bound and dragged to the execution grounds, they demanded that the signboard hung on their backs should be marked with the name "Trotskyist," but this just demand was denied to them. Their mouths were stuffed with cotton to prevent them from shouting at the moment of execution.

From December 1952 to January 1953, wholesale arrests of Trotskyists were staged throughout the country, from Peking to Canton, and from Shanghai to Chung-king. These arrests occurred at midnight of two different days, December 22, 1952, and January 8, 1953. . . .

Up to now we have not yet learned exactly how many were arrested, but there are at least a few hundred already. The victims are not limited to official members of the Trotskyist Party, but include sympathizers and even those who do not have any organizational relations with the party itself except as wives or brothers of Trotskyists.

Since the arrests, the fate of the victims remains an official secret. The families of the arrested went to the Bureau of Public Security to inquire about them, but the only answer they got was, "We are not responsible for this affair; we don't know."[21]

Twenty-five years later, the fate of these working class revolutionists remains an official secret. They have never been brought to trial. If any remain alive, they live still under the regime described by Bao Ruo-wang. There is a recent report that one of the leaders of the Chinese Trotskyists, Cheng Chao-lin, was seen in Shanghai in 1974 in the prison that used to be known as the Ward Road Gaol.

Cheng was a founding member of the Chinese Communist Party as well as of the Chinese Trotskyist movement. He was once a friend of Teng Hsiao-p'ing and Chou En-lai, with whom he worked after the First World War in the first Chinese Communist groups in France. In 1923 he went to Moscow, where he studied at the University of the Toilers of the East. Back in China the next year, he became secretary of the Propaganda Department of the CCP and worked on the party's newspaper, *Guide Weekly*.

Cheng Chao-lin had many skills and talents. He was a linguist, translator, and writer. He spoke French, German, English, and Russian in addition to Chinese. He was the translator of the Chinese edition of the classic *ABC of Communism* by Bukharin and Preobrazhensky. After the revolution of 1926-27 was crushed, he worked in the party underground in Shanghai as editor of the party's main newspaper, *Bolshevik*. He became convinced that Stalin's policy of collaboration with Chiang Kai-shek had led to that terrible defeat for the Chinese working class, and he became a supporter of Leon Trotsky in the battle within the international Communist movement. This led to his expulsion from the party in 1929 along with Ch'en Tu-hsiu, the party's founder, and Peng Shu-tse, another long-time member of the Central Committee and Political Bureau.

In 1931, Cheng was arrested by the Kuomintang. He was seven years in prison. With the twenty-five years given to him by the Stalinists, this devoted working class fighter has spent almost half of his long life in captivity. Even under the most difficult circumstances Cheng revealed both the dedication and the creative energy that the Marxist movement is capable of calling forth in people. Greg Benton, in an article reporting that Cheng had been seen recently, described his activity in the 1940s during his few remaining years of freedom:

He then returned to Shanghai, where he participated in the underground anti-Japanese resistance while continuing his literary activities.

He translated many Marxist works into Chinese, and completed some historical and theoretical studies of his own (including a biography of Ch'en Tu-hsiu and a history of the Chinese reformist movement). He also wrote a novel entitled Dialogue of Three Travellers.[22]

The leaders of the CCP tried to persuade Cheng to capitulate to them in the early 1950s. He refused and was arrested shortly afterward.

A footnote on the morality of the CCP is that in 1975, when Teng Hsiao-p'ing was acting as premier, the government released several hundred Kuomintang officers, who had been jailed in 1949 for war crimes. The Chinese Trotskyists remained.

How many others share their fate? No one knows for certain. In the final chapter of this book we will come to some testimony from recent inmates who remain in China today. Of the others who have written on this, Bao Ruo-wang has this to say:

The estimates of the Chinese forced-labor-camp population vary wildly, depending mostly on the political convictions of the person making the estimate. There are even some distinguished authors, intellectuals and academics in the West who appear to believe that there never was a labor camp or political prisoner in mainland China. At the other extreme are certain Sinologists who affirm that upwards of twenty million are being held in servitude for ideological reasons. Obviously, the Chinese government furnishes no statistics, but I can assure the reader from personal experience that the camps exist and that their population is colossal.[23]

Bao ventures his own estimate:

An interesting hint of the possible scale is contained in a phrase dear to Chinese rhetoricians: "Only a small minority, perhaps five percent, is against us; these are being forced to build socialism." No one who takes a stand against the government can remain out of jail, but if we take only two percent as a reasonable possibility, this still gives us a figure of sixteen million prime candidates for Reform Through Labor. This figure does not include those individuals undergoing the standard three-year terms of *Lao Jiao*—Education Through Labor. These are persons who have committed "mistakes" rather than "crimes." In theory, they maintain their civic rights while in the camps. There are at least as many undergoing *Lao Jiao* as *Lao Gai* [reform through labor]; in fact, probably many more.[24]

Are such figures impossibly high? The "rhetoricians" of the CCP regime continue to use the five percent figure referred to by Bao, even when directly questioned about the scale of the repression that this implies. In a conversation between a Chinese diplomatic official in Peking and *New York Times* columnist William Safire, who had just visited Peking on assignment, the official remarked:

> China is the country where human rights are best observed. Over 95 percent of the population enjoy human rights, and the other 5 percent, if they are receptive to reeducation, they can also enjoy human rights. On the contrary, in the United States only 5 percent of the population enjoys human rights, and 95 percent don't have them.[25]

Five percent of 800 million Chinese is 40 million. Safire asked if this was an actual figure, and if so, who these people were. He was told that the figure was about right, and that it included "landlords, rich peasants, bad elements, counter-revolutionaries and bourgeois revisionists." The official, then thinking further on the matter, added, "Maybe that figure is less."

Since Mao's death and the dismantling of his faction, the Chinese press has for the first time confirmed openly the broad outline of this picture of life under the Mao regime. Though no overall figures have been issued, reports of false arrest, imprisonment, and rural exile for many thousands of people have become common. Often, it is now admitted, reprisals were taken against whole social strata, accused not of any political opposition but of being tainted, as with original sin, by having foreign relatives, having studied science, or having been writers.

In January 1978 the *People's Daily* reported that under the Mao regime—again referred to as the "gang of four"—thousands of Chinese citizens had been systematically persecuted on the sole ground that they had relatives living in other countries. The article promised:

> As to all those who have been subjected to investigation or persecution in the past several years on account of their overseas relations . . . correct conclusions should be drawn . . . so they will be cleared of all slanders and false charges.[26]

In February Hsinhua reported that "hundreds of people" in the Shanghai branch of the Chinese Academy of Sciences had been falsely accused of being agents of the Kuomintang early in the Cultural Revolution in 1967. They had been subjected to "mental torture," "bodily mistreatment," and "fascist savage acts." An investigation at the beginning of 1978 showed that not a single one of the accused was guilty.[27]

In March, Hsinhua reported:

Over 10,000 victims of the "gang of four" have been rehabilitated by the Shanghai Municipal Committee of the Chinese Communist Party. The 10,000 had been persecuted for opposing the gang, and justice has now been done in line with party policy. . . .
Rehabilitation measures include cancelling wrong verdicts, stopping unjust punishment and adjusting improper work assignments. Corrections have also been made in cases of children of persecuted parents who met discrimination when they applied to join the party, the Youth League or the army, or who had trouble entering universities or finding work for which they were suited.[28]

And in May:

Some 300 experienced leaders in cultural work were driven from their posts, revolutionary art associations paralyzed and publications banned. Altogether, over a thousand people under the old Ministry of Culture and its subordinate institutions suffered a wide range of repressions, from branding and expulsion to imprisonment.[29]

Of particular concern to the new leadership is the rehabilitation of the supporters in the party of Liu Shao-ch'i and Teng Hsiao-p'ing who were purged in 1966-69. These victims of the Mao period are themselves largely members of the bureaucracy. A June 1977 issue of *Red Flag,* the CCP's theoretical journal, called on party committees to make it their "major task for the present and for some time to come" to review the cases of such party cadres. Though somewhat guarded, the article is highly suggestive of what happened to these party members, and, under the Maoist usage of guilt by association, to their relatives and co-workers. These are some of the main points:

—cases that have been settled but where there have been unjust verdicts should be corrected and all false charges should be cancelled;
—appropriate work should be allotted to those who can work but still have no work; new positions should be given to those who were allotted inappropriate work; proper arrangements should also be made for the old, weak or disabled, for their political and material welfare;
—realistic conclusions should be drawn for those comrades who died while under investigation and the consequences taken care of;
—the problems caused by the investigation of a person to his innocent family members, descendants, friends and relatives and to those who worked under him should be solved and proper settlements made.[30]

The article gives no figures for the numbers involved, but stresses that "it is not just a few but a large number of cadres who need to have their cases settled." The category of cadre in

China is usually used synonymously with party member, and sometimes extended to other state and economic functionaries who are not members of the party. The party itself has 35 million members. The article adds:

> For a long time, subjectivism and metaphysics were rampant, and party rules and regulations were trampled underfoot and [the] socialist judicial system was followed in random fashion, fascist torture and interrogations were employed and there were large numbers of frame-ups and unjust charges.

Outside of party members, the largest single group of political prisoners to win a reconsideration of their cases since Mao's death has been those branded as rightists in 1957 after the Hundred Flowers Bloom episode. At the end of May 1978 the government quietly let it be known that it was lifting the ban on some one million people who had lost their civil rights, and for the most part been denied work or restricted to the most menial jobs for twenty years. The first week of June this was followed up with the release from the camps of the part of that number who had been imprisoned. The number was reported as 110,000.[31]

Part IV

Mao's Heirs

14. Signs of Instability

It is difficult to weigh the extent of opposition to the Mao regime or to its successor. Not that there is no evidence of such things, but the evidence is scanty and hard to verify. With that caution, no picture of China after Mao would be complete without an attempt to sum up what has happened on this score over the last two years.

There were the massive Hangchow strikes of 1975 and the Tien An Men demonstrations of April 1976. These would not have taken place if there was not significant disaffection among the masses, on both economic and political issues. At the same time there is no indication of any oppositional organization, beyond a few very tiny groups. (I will come back to this in Chapter 16.)

Without broader organization, all protest inevitably takes on individual forms or is limited to spontaneous eruptions. The same is not true of clashes between factions of the bureaucracy, such as resistance by the local supporters of the Mao faction, or possible frictions between Hua's people and other cliques we do not yet know about. These considerations come up in trying to evaluate the reports that filled the Chinese press in November and December 1976 of "civil war" in various provinces.

Certain of the incidents appear to have had a definite factual basis. Both the Chinese press and foreign visitors have confirmed that one of the country's largest tractor factories, located in Kiangsi province, was closed for ten months in 1975-76 as a result of clashes between the workers and management. The official press has claimed that the clashes were inspired by the "gang of four," but it is not possible to verify this assertion.

November 1976 broadcasts from Fukien reported in effect that martial law had been declared in that coastal province:

. . . the party committee of the People's Liberation Army units on the Fukien front has organized large numbers of commanders and fighters into propaganda and mass work teams and dispatched them to various cities, rural villages, factories, mines, government offices, schools and neighborhoods of our province to vigorously support local work and enthusiastically propagate the instructions of the party Central Committee.[1]

Although the reports in the Chinese press and on provincial radio broadcasts appeared after the fall of the Mao faction, many of them professed to describe clashes that had taken place earlier, in the spring and early summer of 1976, which were not part of the post-Mao purge battles. One series of radio broadcasts from the major industrial center of Wuhan, in Hupeh province, described how the area had been "thrown into chaos," supposedly by the machinations of the "gang of four." The broadcasts, monitored in December 1976, claimed that the four purged leaders "created white terror, split the ranks of the working class, incited armed struggles, (and) killed and wounded class brothers."[2]

In Honan province, just north of Hupeh, rebellious forces were said to have "stormed organs of the dictatorship of the proletariat and the provincial and lower-level party committees," according to a December 7 broadcast. A December 9 broadcast mentioned similar turmoil in Yunnan province.

The *New York Times* reported the following broadcast from Szechwan province, the largest province in China, with a population of 80 million:

Because of sabotage by the gang of four, civil war and factionalism did not cease in our province. Many class brothers . . . were sacrificed in all-round civil war. Armed struggle was protracted and large in scale, and people's lives and property suffered serious loss.[3]

According to a radio broadcast from Shansi province, "the black hands of the gang of four in our province, in a planned and premeditated way, caused the incident of beating, wrecking and looting on Aug. 23, kidnapping and beating up the principal leading comrades of the provincial party committee."[4]

The most dramatic incident of this kind took place in the industrial city of Paoting, a major railroad junction a hundred miles south of Peking. It was also the one case where official documents provided any details of what was supposed to have happened. The clashes in Paoting began months before the fall of the "gang of four." They were referred to frequently in the Chinese press after October, but only in general terms. The specific details come from a Central Committee proclamation issued in October 1976, a copy of which was obtained by Western diplomats in Peking. The document said that a handful of "class enemies" had incited people to

> fight, smash, and rob all over the place, robbing military arsenals, banks, grain stores, shops and so on, stealing state property, collective and individual property; disrupting communications and telecommunications, and interrupting the supply of earthquake relief goods to Tangshan.
>
> These people stopped military vehicles, blew up factories, sabotaged and arrested others, murdered, and raped. There was no evil they didn't stoop to.

The proclamation demanded that

> fighting groups of all description are to be disbanded, all bases and checkpoints are to be disbanded, and all weapons, ammunitions and explosives which have been stolen, manufactured, and hidden away in the community are to be handed in at collection points directed by troops. . . . All persons detained by armed groups are to be released.[5]

Clearly there were big disturbances in Fukien and Paoting, at least, though the numerous other accounts lack outside witnesses or other substantiating evidence. But what actually happened, what forces were involved, and what their aims were remains clouded. Months after the event, the *Far Eastern Economic Review* said that in Paoting "peasants ran amok and raided granaries and arsenals."[6]

What is clear is that following the disturbances of the summer and fall of 1976, the government lashed out with a wave of public executions, for both "political" and ordinary crimes. These unquestionably took place, with witnesses to the parading of the victims in Canton in April 1977, and many foreign observers of the official execution orders posted in major cities. In April 1977 *Le Monde* gave a total of about fifty for those shot in March and the first two weeks of April.[7] The total comes from posted notices seen by foreign visitors, to whom most of the country still remains off limits. The executions took place in Wuhan, Hangchow, Shanghai, Changsha, and Shenyang.

After many such killings in the Cultural Revolution, the public notices of such things had become rare. A sequence of this magnitude in a few months' time strongly suggests deliberate national policy. In fact, the first such executions were reported shortly after Hua took power at the end of 1976. They were the executions of two people in Changsha, capital of Hunan province:

a man, for defacing a wall poster with Hua's name on it; and a woman, accused of prostitution.[8]

The killings did not stop in April. In May eight people were sentenced to death in Shenyang, in Northeast China. One of these cases was different from most of the others in the kinds of charges made against the victims. In the other reported cases, about half of those shot were accused of supporting the "gang of four," and the other half were accused of nonpolitical crimes, such as financial speculation, etc. In the Shenyang case, one was charged with "listening to an enemy radio" and "founding a counterrevolutionary party." No details were provided, but the party was reportedly called the Chinese Revolutionary Party, and the "enemy radio" was supposed to have been in the USSR, not on Taiwan as might have been expected.[9] Twelve alleged partisans of the "gang of four" were shot in Anyang, Honan province, on August 2.[10] Ross Munro, writing from Peking in November, added:

> More than 30 people were executed here and in the Yunnan provincial capital of Kunming last month for political or criminal activities, according to court notices seen recently by foreigners.
>
> This brings to almost 200 the number of executions which foreign observers have documented in China since the new "moderate" leadership came to power one year ago. The information documenting the latest and nearly all the other cases of executions comes from official notices issued by local courts and posted on buildings.
>
> Since foreigners have seen only a small percentage of all the court notices which must have been posted in this country during the past year, some observers have calculated on the basis of the 200 documented executions that the total number is several thousand. . . .
>
> One court notice seen in Kunming last month listed 47 names and singled out 23 of these as the names of people who had been sentenced to immediate execution. Most of the 23 condemned—some of whom were women—were shot for political reasons. They were charged with such crimes as distributing counter-revolutionary literature and forming counter-revolutionary groups.[11]

The communist movement before the advent of Stalinism stood unanimous in its opposition to the use of the death penalty as an instrument of judicial punishment. Morality, of course, is not ahistorical or above classes. Fighters for working class emancipation have a special interest in opposing the use of the death penalty under capitalism because this is a weapon used by the capitalist minority to terrorize the workers and to secure its rule.

But this does not mean, as the Stalinists would argue, that while it is wrong for capitalists to kill workers it is right for the workers' state to kill "enemies of the people." We are speaking here of the use of capital punishment as a routine sanction, and not about times of civil war and revolution when the rules of war apply. The use of this measure by the Stalinists is all the more to be condemned, however, in that its main victims are working people.

The use of judicial murder in peacetime is the hallmark of a regime based on minority rule, on privilege, which must use terror in some form to sustain itself. What is taking place in China today is not a matter of the working class meting out punishment to its adversaries, but of the privileged bureaucracy using force and violence to suppress the workers and peasants over whom it rules. This spectacle is particularly revolting when these killings are not even reserved for acts that everyone can agree are antisocial crimes, such as murder and rape, but are meted out to people for trying to assert their rights or to victims of the social system. Prostitution, listening to the radio, distributing a leaflet, speaking words that the bureaucracy has decided are counterrevolutionary—in what medieval mind do these things merit death as a punishment?

In truth, the resort to such methods reveals a deep inner weakness of the bureaucracy, not its strength and resolution. The masters must be very afraid if they must kill people for such things lest they be brought down.

15. The New Party Leadership

The consolidation of a new leadership group—for the time being at least—was announced publicly with the convening of the Eleventh Congress of the CCP in Peking, August 12 to 18, 1977. The congress contained few surprises, but it did offer a hint of the lineup in the post-Mao era. It also revealed the extent of the purge of Mao's personal faction, which was not by any means limited to the "gang of four."

After almost thirty years in power, the CCP still conducts its deliberations as though it were a persecuted opposition—in complete secrecy. The Chinese people discovered that their ruling party was holding a congress only after it was over, when the announcement was released to the press on August 20. There was, as usual, no publication beforehand of any documents that could provide a basis for discussion by the party's members.

Constitutionally, the party congress is the highest decision-making body of the CCP and the forum where the ranks have the opportunity to set policy and elect the leadership. This fiction has a ludicrous side to it when the interval between congresses is prolonged to the point that the previous congress decisions, presumably still binding on the leadership, remain unreviewed for many years.

Thus, the main decision of the Seventh Congress, in 1945, was to instruct the party leadership to seek a coalition government with Chiang Kai-shek. This remained in force until the next congress was held—in 1956, seven years after Chiang was overthrown.

The Eighth Congress in 1956 gave its endorsement to Khrushchev's speech condemning Stalin, a speech which Peking later claimed had "restored capitalism" in the USSR. That was not reviewed by a party congress until 1969, almost a decade after Khrushchev had become a target of abuse in the Chinese press.

The Ninth Congress in 1969 made Defense Minister Lin Piao

the official successor to Mao Tsetung, even writing this into the party constitution. That constitution remained in force until 1973, two years after Lin had been killed after allegedly trying to assassinate Mao.

The Tenth Congress in 1973 marked the consolidation of Mao's personal faction, now rid of Lin Piao, in both policy and personnel. By the time of the opening of the Eleventh Congress in August 1977, many of the policies adopted four years earlier were being denounced as "fascist" and a large section of the top party leadership promoted by Mao was under arrest.

The new congress had a limited agenda: a political report, which took the form of a four-hour speech by party Chairman Hua Kuo-feng; the adoption of a new party constitution, reported on by seventy-nine-year-old Defense Minister Yeh Chien-ying; the election of a new Central Committee and Politburo; and a brief closing address by Teng Hsiao-p'ing. (Teng had finally been officially rehabilitated in July.)

The press communiqué issued by Hsinhua said that Hua had stressed in his report that "Mao Tsetung Thought is a new acquisition enriching the treasure-house of Marxist-Leninist theory and is Chairman Mao's most precious legacy to our era."[1]

The summary of Hua's speech was, however, a repudiation of virtually all of the specific campaigns initiated by Mao in the last ten years of his life. Hua declared that the Cultural Revolution had come to a "triumphant conclusion"—with the arrest of the "gang of four," who with Mao had been its principal leaders!

He added that

this has ushered in a new period of development in our country's socialist revolution and socialist construction. Now we are able to achieve stability and unity and attain great order across the land in compliance with Chairman Mao's instructions.[2]

What Hua here called Mao's "instructions" were, of course, nothing of the sort. As everyone in China recalled, when Mao denounced Teng Hsiao-p'ing as a "representative of the bourgeoisie" in April 1976, it was because Teng allegedly failed to make "class struggle" the "key link" ahead of "stability and unity."

While China's problems were not openly discussed at Hua's handpicked congress, concern over them was reflected in the leadership changes that took place there. In China the actual power is centered not in the congress, nor even in the Central Committee, but in the Politburo and its elite Standing Committee.

Some Western reporters noted the high degree of continuity

from the remaining members of the Tenth Politburo to the Eleventh, which is in contrast to an extensive new purge of the Central Committee itself, revealed for the first time in the list published after the Eleventh Congress. This appearance of continuity is misleading, since the purge in this important body was carried out long ago, right after the death of Mao. The decimation of Mao's faction in the Politburo can be seen in the contrast between the number of them included in the full Politburo of 1973 and those who were still on hand to stand for reelection in 1977.

On the eve of the Eleventh Congress, of the five vice-chairmen elected at the Tenth Congress, only two remained—Yeh Chien-ying, and Li Te-sheng, the military commander of Manchuria and a former hard Maoist. Of these, Li was dropped from his vice-chairmanship by the new congress.

Of the nine members of the Politburo Standing Committee elected in 1973, only two remained in 1977; again, Yeh and Li. (Chairman Hua was not considered important enough in 1973 to be elected to the Standing Committee.)

Only twelve of the twenty-two members of the full Politburo were still around by August 1977, the rest either dead of old age or under arrest.

The situation in the 195-member Central Committee (enlarged by the August congress to 201) was quite different. The list published in August was the first indication of who had survived the purge of the Mao faction. No fewer than 85 of the 195 CC members elected in 1973 were dropped. Allowing for the six known deaths among these, that still comes to about 40 percent of the party leadership.[3]

Those dropped were overwhelmingly the relatively young representatives of "mass organizations" used by Mao in the Cultural Revolution as a cudgel to beat the veteran bureaucracy into line. Their replacements are the same aged administrators Mao accused of "capitalist restorationism" in 1966.

This move should not be misunderstood as having anything to do with making the new CC less—or more—democratic or representative. It is true that most of Mao's model workers and peasants have been dropped from the committee. But it would be mistaken to equate them with actual representatives of the masses. Their elevation at the party congresses in 1969 and 1973 was tied to the rise of the Mao cult and its peculiar adaptation of reactionary Chinese ruling class traditions to the administration of the Chinese workers' state. They were chosen for their personal loyalty to the chairman, not to the masses they ostensibly represented.

Moreover, like the so-called gang of four, who epitomized this faction in the party, the "model workers and peasants" were among the most ignorant zealots of the bureaucracy.

It is not surprising, then, that Mao's faction has been swept away by the remainder of the bureaucracy. The significant point is that these functionaries have nothing to offer as substitutes but their own aging corps of survivors of the Cultural Revolution. The *average* age of the new twenty-three-member Politburo is sixty-eight, which makes it about the oldest party leadership anywhere in the world.

The "new" faces on the Politburo included such figures as Hsu Hsiang-ch'ien, 75, and Nieh Jung-chen, 78, two of China's army marshalls; head of the Academy of Sciences Fang I, 68; foreign trade expert Keng Piao, 68; Yu Ch'iu-li, 63, head of the national planning commission; and Su Chen-hua, 68, an admiral purged by Mao in 1966 who is now in charge of cleaning Mao's appointees out of their former stronghold in Shanghai. The youngest member of the new Politburo, and the only one under 50, was Ni Chih-fu, 44, a specialist in questions of public order and former head of the Peking militia, who was in Shanghai reorganizing the militia there.

In the official rankings, the holdovers from the previous committee retained the top posts. Hua Kuo-feng succeeded at this congress in "legitimizing" his hold on the chairmanship, which until then rested on a scribbled note by Mao in which the dying chairman said that he was "at ease" with Hua taking care of some provincial problems. The four vice-chairmen are Defense Minister Yeh Chien-ying, Teng Hsiao-p'ing, economic planner Li Hsien-nien, and Wang Tung-hsing, the commander of the leadership's private bodyguard troops and director of the General Office of the Central Committee.

Among the most prominent of the remaining members reelected to the Politburo are Ch'en Hsi-lien, commander of the Peking military region, and Wu Te, the capital's mayor; and in Canton, party secretary Wei Kuo-ch'ing and Kwangtung military commander Hsu Shih-yu.

The pair from Peking, Ch'en and Wu, were particularly close to the "gang of four" before Mao's death. Wu gave the order over Peking radio for the dispersal of the Tien An Men demonstrations, and Ch'en commanded the troops that carried out the suppression. The two have been publicly attacked in wall posters on several occasions in 1977 and 1978, demanding their removal from office and their punishment for their role at Tien An Men. It is not clear at this time whether these attacks emanate from genuine oppositionists to the new government or from the people around Teng Hsiao-p'ing, who also suffered reprisals at the hands of Mao and his lieutenants after Tien An Men.

In the next level, the full Central Committee, the most notable addition was the rehabilitation of Lo Jui-ch'ing, once the head of the secret police. Lo was chief of staff of the People's Liberation Army when he was purged in 1966. It was Lo, it will be recalled, who explained to the First National People's Congress back in 1954 the assistance of Soviet advisers in the establishment of the CCP's labor camp system.

The composition is clear. The new leadership consists of aged military men, technicians, police, city administrators, foreign-trade experts, economists, and planners.

Mao was fond of saying that in China, women hold up half of heaven. His successors have not lived up to his saying in dispensing the posts of power on earth. Not one single woman was included in the twenty-three-member Politburo. In the Central Committee, the twenty who were elected in 1973 were cut back to fourteen out of 201, or 7 percent.

The party congress was followed by the convening of the Fifth National People's Congress (NPC), China's nominal parliament, in Peking February 26–March 5, 1978. This was generally a cut-and-dried affair, part of the show of national unity around the new leadership. Hua Kuo-feng was reelected to the post of premier, which he holds concurrently with the position of CCP chairman. Yeh Chien-ying retired as head of the armed forces and became the chairman of the NPC, an honorific post that has few duties or powers. He was replaced as defense minister by Hsu Hsiang-ch'ing, a seventy-five-year-old veteran of the Long March.

The congress had two themes: industrial modernization and the search for popular support for the new regime, under the slogan of giving "full play to people's democracy." These campaigns were concretized in the adoption of a ten-year plan (counting from 1975, when the previous five-year plan was supposed to have begun but didn't), and a new national constitution.

Only two of the targets of the economic plan were made public. Hua promised a grain harvest in 1985 of 400 million metric tons and the production of steel in that same year of 60 million tons.[4] Both of these targets require a substantially greater increase in overall output in the next seven years than has been achieved in the whole of the last twenty. There was no indication of how they were to be achieved.

The new constitution replaced one adopted only three years earlier at the previous NPC. In general the new document was closer to the original constitution of the People's Republic of 1954, in that it restored the promise of many democratic rights that were simply deleted in 1975 and in its restoration of the (purely formal) separation of party and state, which had also been done away with in the 1975 document.

Though not much in the spotlight at these official gatherings, the most important figure in the new regime next to Hua was Teng Hsiao-p'ing. At the Eleventh Party Congress he regained the posts of chief of staff of the army, vice-chairman of the CCP, and vice-premier of the government. In February, while the NPC was meeting, a concurrent session was called of the moribund Chinese People's Political Consultative Conference, China's advisory coalition government composed of those capitalist parties and politicians that chose not to follow Chiang Kai-shek to Taiwan back in 1949. This meeting of fossils of Chinese capitalism elected Teng as its chairman.

16. The Case of Li I-che

What does the future hold in China? The emergence of a post-Mao gerontocracy is only part of the answer, and far from the most important part. Even before Mao departed there had begun to be changes, a new mood of independence from the bureaucratic hierarchy. The Hangchow strikes in the summer of 1975 and the Tien An Men demonstrations were the most dramatic evidence of this process. Smaller, less tangible, changes were also taking place.

The death of Mao was in some ways like the breaking up of a logjam, in which the waters of social life, dammed up and stagnant, began to flow again. Many sufferers breathed a great sigh of relief when the unpredictable old tyrant was finally laid to rest. This may be disputed by the cultists. And it may have appeared somewhat muted in the initial shock that his reign was over. But there is no misinterpreting the joyful explosion when Mao's henchmen finally fell.*

Hua Kuo-feng's promises of reform are themselves a symptom of a shift in the relations between the bureaucracy and the masses. And while the leadership has given little, people have begun to act—in small ways—differently than they would have a few years ago. Reporter Fox Butterfield describes a scene in a Peking movie theater during a showing of the film *Woman Pilot*:

---

* Harrison Salisbury discussed this with one of the present editors of the Shanghai daily *Wen Wei Bao,* Chu Hsi-chi. Chu had been imprisoned by the Mao regime from 1968 until the day the "gang of four" fell, when he ran away from the pig farm where he had been sentenced to work, returned to Shanghai, and was put in charge of reorganizing the newspaper he had been purged from. Chu described Shanghai the night after the news of the arrest of Chiang Ch'ing: "That night I was with my friends celebrating the arrest of the Gang of Four. We stayed up all night drinking. So did 10 million other people in Shanghai. By morning every bottle of mai tai and rice wine in the liquor stores had been consumed" (*New York Times Magazine,* December 4, 1977).

At a critical moment, a male pilot, who has established "a close comradely relationship" with the heroine, dies in a training accident.

Informed by her friends, she bursts into tears. Then, suddenly catching herself, the heroine intones solemnly: "It's nothing. It is all for the revolution."

At this sentiment, the audience breaks into howls of laughter.[1]

To dare to laugh at the regime's absurdly imposed conventions is like a breath of fresh air in a stale room. It is not revolutionary; but it is a sign that the bureaucracy is not all-powerful.

Even more hopeful are the signs of a small but determined opposition that has grown up since the end of the Cultural Revolution. To openly oppose the government brings great risks. As we have seen, it can mean immediate execution. At the least it means arrest and the camps. Yet there are young Chinese rebels today who face that threat without flinching and stand up to the government. They have set an example that has had a deep impact in China, far out of proportion to their numbers.

The most famous of these revolutionary opponents of Chinese Stalinism today is Li I-che, the pen name of three former Red Guards from Canton, Li Cheng-t'ien, Ch'en I-yang, and Wang Hsi-che. Li Cheng-t'ien, the leader of the group, was a graduate student at the Canton Art Institute in 1966 when the Cultural Revolution began. A loyal supporter of Chairman Mao, he joined the Red Guards and became a leader of the Red Revolt Headquarters organization in Canton. At the end of the Cultural Revolution, when the Red Guard groups were suppressed, Li was arrested and spent two years in jail. He was released in 1971, after the purge of Lin Piao.

Li reflected for a long time on the politics of China. While not abandoning his personal belief in Mao, he came to reject the bureaucratic system of Chinese Stalinism. In the summer of 1973, he and his comrades began work on a pamphlet entitled *Concerning Socialist Democracy and the Legal System*. It was drafted as an appeal to the upcoming Fourth National People's Congress. The congress, however, was long delayed and did not take place until January 1975.

In the meantime, Li completed a second draft of his article in December 1973, and a final draft, with a long introduction, dated November 7, 1974. The Li I-che group then cut stencils of the pamphlet to be used as a wall poster—actually almost a small book—so that multiple copies could be made. It has since circulated in various parts of China as "samizdat" literature.

In December 1974 the courageous trio pasted up a copy of their poster on Peking Road in Canton. It ran a hundred yards in length, and took sixty-seven sheets of newsprint for the whole text. Crowds gathered to read and copy it.

The authorities reacted indecisively. For several weeks they permitted the poster to remain in place. An account of what followed has been published, along with the text, by young radical Chinese in Hong Kong in the book *The Revolution Is Dead, Long Live the Revolution.* The editors write:

> According to some sources, the local Maoist cadres were stunned by the poster; and they referred the incident and the contents of the poster to the CCP Central Committee for instruction. Li Hsien-nien, vice-premier of the State Council of Communist China, handed down his verdict that the poster was "Reactionary through and through, vicious and malicious to the extreme."
>
> The fate of the author was thus sealed. Public security authorities in Canton put [Li Cheng-t'ien] under arrest and temporarily detained him. As a counterrevolutionary culprit and a "negative teacher," Li was brought to various units and mass meetings for public criticism and humiliation. He was also required to write reports of self-criticism for perusal by the authorities.
>
> Since the poster has been so influential and has generated so much debate, a simple self-criticism by Li was, in the opinion of Communist authorities, not sufficient to put the matter to rest. Following past examples, another orthodox poster under the pseudonym of Hsüan Chi-wen appeared in Canton, which was supposed to deliver a coup de grace to Li I-che, or the Li Cheng-t'ien group, and his poster. Although the orthodox criticism was probably penned out by the Propaganda Department of the CCPCC—the highest official organ for dealing with such matters—the quality appeared much inferior to the poster of Li I-che.[2]

What is the content of the Li I-che wall poster? The authors plainly received the whole of their political education in the Maoist movement—in the Cultural Revolution in particular. They remained personally loyal to Mao Tsetung, and accept his word for everything they have not seen with their own eyes. They quote Stalin favorably against Trotsky, repeat the notion that capitalism has been restored in the Soviet Union and Eastern Europe, that Liu Shao-ch'i was an agent of a new bourgeoisie, etc. These things seem in their article to be matters of faith rather than knowledge. However, their article takes on a very different tone when they begin to discuss the political life of the Chinese people in the years since the Cultural Revolution. Now they are on the home ground of their own experience. And through the fog of Mao quotations and obscure slogans left over from the campaigns of the last decade emerges a moving appeal of people who are at heart rebels and fighters for democracy.

Because of their belief that Mao was a defender of the Chinese working class, they identify the regime that emerged from the Cultural Revolution with Lin Piao. Of course, by 1973-74, Lin was dead. The Li I-che document thus refers to "The Lin Piao System," which they feel is being perpetuated in China by the bureaucrats who remained after Lin was gone. They write:

> What has been commonly observed is that some leaders have expanded the necessary preferential treatment granted by the Party and the people into political and economic special privileges, and then extended them boundlessly to their families and clansmen, relatives and friends, even to the degree of exchanging special privileges [among themselves], of obtaining for their children factual inheritance of political and economic positions. . . .[3]

They give some examples of what they mean by the "Lin Piao system"—more accurately the Mao regime, with and without Lin—following the Cultural Revolution:

> We have not forgotten the giving prominence to (empty) politics which rewarded the lazy and punished the diligent, the "daily reading [of Mao's works and quotations]" which resembled the incantation of spells, the "discussion-application [of Mao's works and thoughts]" which became more and more hypocritical . . . the "manifestation of loyalty" which encouraged political speculation, the grotesque "loyalty dance," and the excruciatingly multitudinous rituals of showing loyalty—morning prayers, evening penitences, rallies . . . which were invariably painted with violent religious colors and shrouded in such an atmosphere. In short, loyalty occupied one hundred percent of the time and one hundred percent of the space. . . .

> More so, we have not forgotten the formula "preachings" of class struggle, and the "scum hole" type of cow pens [meaning the detention camps] which were more so and no less [inhuman] than the massacre[s] . . . because in Kwangtung Province alone nearly 40,000 revolutionary masses and cadres were massacred and more than a million revolutionary cadres and masses were imprisoned, put under control, and struggled against.

> But there are some people who shut their eyes and do not admit the fact that the Lin Piao system, which has been witnessed by 800 million people, has been firmly set up; and with thickened faces they stubbornly say that Chairman Mao's revolutionary line has, "at all times and in all places," occupied the ruling position. Is this not to say that all these bloody butcheries and unreversible cases of long standing are based on decisions made by the "revolutionary line"?

Li Cheng-t'ien and his comrades argue that the source of such violations of socialist democracy and legality lie in the privileged position of the central core of the bureaucracy. While some of the sycophantic extremes of the late 1960s have abated, the central administrators in 1973-74 continue the basic antidemocratic practices of the "Lin Piao" period:

The diehards who have insisted on the Lin Piao System have sworn that they will not let the Communists who were struck down by them rise again from the dirt. For this, they have found a knack of doing things, that is, to use "not necessarily available" incriminating evidence [i.e., "evidence" that does not have to be revealed to anyone but the judges— L.E.] to accuse the revolutionary comrades who are more dangerous to them because they [the diehards] can accuse them of being "big counter-revolutionary black hands," "bad counterrevolutionary chieftains," . . . "active counterrevolutionary elements" and "traitors" etc. When they fail to produce evidence against others after protracted periods of imprisonment and licentious maltreatment, they confuse a clear case further into an insolvable mess and then use this as an excuse to continue the case for yet a longer time, waiting for a chance to try again. Are not a great number of cases just so?[5]

The document demands the reopening of the thousands of cases of unjustly imprisoned or executed people of recent years:

May not the hundreds and thousands of framed cases both in the Central and the local areas, which were fabricated by Lin Piao and his cohorts, be reversed and redressed? Can not great numbers of veteran cadres who committed this or that mistake but have proven loyal to the Party through a protracted test be employed again? . . .

The number of people who were put to death by the Lin Piao line was not limited to a few hundreds or thousands. Since veteran revolutionary cadres who had passed their forties and experienced all sorts of hardships were put to death, then how could a girl of only fifteen years old survive? . . .[6]

The Li I-che appeal is directed to the delegates of the then-pending Fourth National People's Congress, "regardless that we do not know how they are elected." It raises a number of specific demands. First of all, the restoration (in reality, the creation) of a genuine legal system in which citizens have definite rights and must be tried under written laws before they can be jailed:

In the summer of 1968, the socialist legal system "suddenly became inoperative," while, on the other hand, "the state power is the power to suppress" became operative. All across the land, there were arrests everywhere, suppressions everywhere, miscarriages of justice everywhere. Where did the socialist legal system go? Allegedly, it was no longer of any use because it belonged to the Constitution established by the old People's Congress whereas the new People's Congress was not convened yet. Now, there was no law and no heaven![7]

Specifically:

The "4th National People's Congress" should stipulate in black and white that all the democratic rights which the masses of people deserve should be protected, and that dictatorship will only be exercised over the criminals who committed murder, arson, gangsterism, robbery and theft and the elements who incited armed struggles and organized conspiratorial cliques.[8]

Second: "Restriction on special privileges."

We are not Utopian socialists; therefore, we acknowledge that there exist in our society at the present stage various kinds of differences which cannot be eliminated by a single law or decree. But, the law governing the development of the socialist revolutionary movement is not to enhance the differences but to eliminate them, and more, so not to allow these differences to be expanded into economic and political privileges. Special privileges are fundamentally opposite to the interests of the people. Why should we be so shy about the criticism of special privileges? . . . [9]

Third: "Guarantee of the people's right of management of the state and the society." This section demanded the right of the people to dismiss "at any time" high officials who "have lost the trust of the broad masses of people."[10]

Fourth: "Consolidation of the dictatorship of the proletariat and sanction against reactionaries." This section read in part:

Are the people's democratic rights not written in our Constitution and Party Constitution and Central documents? Yes, they have been written down. Not only that, but there also are the stipulations of "protecting the people's democracy," "not allowing malicious attack and revenge," and "forbidding extracting a confession by torture and interrogation." But, these protections have been, in fact, always unavailable, while, on the contrary, Fascist dictatorship has been "allowed" to be practiced over the revolutionary cadres and masses—some of them were imprisoned, some executed, and some framed in fabricated cases; even the unlimited practice of savagely corporal punishments cannot be "strictly forbidden."

The "4th National People's Congress" should stipulate in black and white the terms to punish the "ministers" who have committed the heinous crimes of transgressing the law knowingly, violating the law while enforcing it, creating fabricated cases, using the public to avenge personal grudges, establishing special cases without authorization, instituting prisons without authorization, using unlimited corporal punishment, and practicing wanton murder.[11]

Fifth: "Taking concrete measures to ensure the fulfillment of policies." This section protests the arbitrary shifting of party line after a decision has been made, leaving party officials unaccountable for their actions.

And sixth: "From each according to his ability, to each according to his work." The title of this section does not really encompass its content, which is worth looking at closely:

Since the summer of 1968, and owing to suppression of democratic rights in the political sphere, especially by Lin Piao's Fascist organizational line and their nepotism as well as personnel transfers and reshuffles of the disobedient based on punitivism, the principles of "from each according to his ability" and "employ only the competent" have been sabotaged and the people's socialist initiative trampled underfoot.

At the same time when we see that the special privileges are expanding we also see clearly that the worker and peasant laboring masses are deprived of many of their reasonable economic benefits under slogans of "public property-ism." For many years, the workers have not had their wages raised, but had the reasonable monetary rewards which were part of their wages abolished; while the peasants suffered even greater losses as a result of the movements of [turning in] uncompensated "loyalty grains," high quota requisitioning of grain, and "cutting off the tail of private ownership." . . . [12]

This is a powerful indictment of the Mao regime, coming from inside China, and even from young communist rebels who continue to cling to the forlorn illusion that someone else, and not Mao, was responsible for the conditions they describe. They formulate from their own experience many of the central demands of the coming antibureaucratic political revolution in China. They have not yet drawn the full conclusions from what they have seen. That is evident in part by singling out the summer of 1968 as the date when things went bad for democracy in China. Li Cheng-t'ien and his comrades came to political life only two years before that, inspired by the radical democratic rhetoric Mao employed to mobilize youth such as them against his factional opponents in the party leadership. But what they call the Lin Piao system was not Lin's particular creation. It was and is endemic to the Stalinist bureaucratic caste.

There is a postscript to the appeal of Li I-che. In 1975, Li

Cheng-t'ien, Ch'en I-yang, and Wang Hsi-che were put on trial in Canton. By all accounts the three conducted themselves bravely and refused to concede the government's claim that *Concerning Socialist Democracy and the Legal System* was a traitorous or criminal document. Their trial was held before a "mass" court, in which the "masses" are selected by the prosecution, and conviction is a foregone conclusion. Nevertheless, in a surprise reaction, the jurors remained silent throughout the proceedings and refused to either repeat the prosecutor's criticisms of the defendants or to vote for a conviction. Lacking any official conviction, the three were then arbitrarily sentenced to a term of "labor reform" in a tungsten mine outside of Canton.

After the fall of Chiang Ch'ing and the Mao faction, the new government, promising an end to such arbitrary arrests, reopened the Li I-che case. The new verdict was not what the government's promises might have led one to expect. Li Cheng-t'ien, Ch'en I-yang, and Wang Hsi-che were reportedly arrested at the tungsten mine where they worked in December 1976 and declared counterrevolutionaries.[13]

A confirmation of this report appeared in the *Far Eastern Economic Review*: "A recent visitor to Canton saw an official announcement posted on the doors of the Supreme Court of Kwangtung province that Li had been sentenced to 'indefinite imprisonment.' The fate of his co-authors . . . remains unknown."[14]

Since the end of the Cultural Revolution and the suppression of the Red Guard movement, more than 10,000 former Red Guards have fled China and settled in Hong Kong. Unlike earlier waves of refugees, most of these were the children of party members, frequently industrial workers. In May 1976 a group of these former Red Guards, who remain socialists, began publication of *Yellow River* magazine in Hong Kong. Modeled on the *Chronicle of Current Events* published by Soviet dissidents, this magazine concentrates on the publication of underground literature and the defense of political prisoners in China. It has recently joined forces with a group of radical Chinese exiles from Taiwan who publish the magazine *Wild Grass (Yeh Ts'ao)* in the United States. The Hong Kong based group has also formed the Chinese Human Rights Society.

The Chinese Trotskyists in Hong Kong have been active in the defense of political prisoners and have initiated demonstrations and conferences that have united a number of organizations on the Hong Kong Left. They publish two monthly magazines,

October Review (Shih Yueh P'ing-lun) and *Equator (Ch'ih Tao)*.

In the spring of 1977, the former Red Guards who publish *Yellow River* launched an international appeal on behalf of the authors of the Li I-che wall poster. The Chinese Human Rights Society and the Hong Kong Chinese Trotskyist organizations have helped circulate the appeal throughout the world.

The appeal also demanded the release of Yang Hsi-kuang, a Hunan leader of the left-wing Great Proletarian Revolutionary Alliance and author of the oppositionist document *Whither China?* of the late 1960s. Yang has been in prison in China since 1967.

The world appeal declared in part:

Was Li I-che arrested for having lifted a corner of brocade curtain to uncover the spectacle of bloody repression that marked the end of the Great Cultural Revolution? But these are things that no Chinese will ever be able to forget, even if they send them all to jail.

Was Li I-che arrested for having demanded that socialist democracy be established and the people's constitutional rights respected, so that the masses could at last have a little room to breathe, and so that they could express themselves and act according to laws, and not according to the whims of a few leaders?

Is this what is considered so unbearable, such a provocation, by the authorities, whether they represent one "system" or another one? But if it is still a crime today to speak of socialist democracy and the people's constitutional rights, whose interests are served by the establishment of "peace and order in the country"? What good does it do to brag about a "new stage of socialism"?

Was Li I-che arrested precisely because he disturbed the peace of the leaders by expressing his justified concern over the crisis wracking Chinese society today, his fears for the future of the country, and his sincere solicitude for people's living conditions? . . .

Is it perhaps precisely because Li I-che said out loud what the people are forbidden to say? Because he let out a shout of anger at a time when the people had had enough of stepping back, giving in, and being patient, just as he had? . . . There were numerous "fearless" young people, "survivors" of the repression, sent to prison or to labor camps merely because they disturbed the peace of the leaders. They have not abandoned and will not abandon their concern for the people and their hope for a better society—not yesterday, not today, and not tomorrow!

We who spent our childhood and youth in China cannot let them remain forgotten.[15]

17. A Look Ahead

In the appeal for Li I-che by the exiled Red Guards, the word *survivors* appears in quotation marks. That is because it is a special word in the vocabulary of the Chinese people. It is a word one hears often from those who have grown up in China in this century. It should not be mistaken for passivity. The tradition of rebellion in China runs deep and goes back to the dawn of recorded history. If it has yet to succeed in its eventual aim, which today can only mean socialist liberation through the overthrow of the bureaucracy by the Chinese masses themselves, neither has their sense of justice ever been fully crushed. Their resilience, pride, and discipline to some degree deflect every blow that is not fatal, in line with the saying that what does not kill me makes me stronger.

These characteristics give to Chinese political life a dual quality. If in ordinary times it is conformist and repressive, great reserves of anger are stored away, savored even, against that day when retribution will be possible. This makes Chinese politics—like American politics—very violent. Hua Kuo-feng has locked up Li Cheng-t'ien. Other Li Cheng-t'iens have died on the execution grounds at Hua's command. Both Hua and his henchmen must worry sometimes. Why are there always more of these "survivors" who just don't understand the relationship of forces, who unreasonably refuse to participate in the ritual of confession?

The workers and peasants of China once gave their trust to Hua's party and its leadership. They fought and sacrificed to defeat Japanese imperialism and in their revolution against Chiang Kai-shek, with a heroism that inspired the world. The bureaucracy has sought to claim for itself the credit and rewards of all this, even when it intones the maxim that "the masses are the real makers of history." The Stalinists will discover, to their pain and disadvantage, that on this point, at least, they are right.

The masses are the real makers of history. Though not while

they are atomized and directionless, it is true. Groups like Li I-che have already begun to formulate a program of action, to put forward many of the demands of the antibureaucratic revolution. When this is joined to organization, the power of the bureaucratic caste can be broken. Not just any sort of organization can accomplish this task. The bureaucracy mimics the forms of Leninist party organization and deforms them to serve its ends. A genuine Leninist party, of the kind the Bolsheviks had under Lenin and Trotsky, is a powerful and indispensable weapon in the fight for liberation. Until such a party is forged by the Chinese masses, the bureaucracy, with its superior organization, retains a telling advantage in the combat.

This will not be an easy or a short fight. The bureaucracy claws for its existence with a savagery that is proportional to the benefits that it derives from its parasitic way of life. But the mass of "survivors" are many and the bureaucracy is ultimately few. Its incapacity to solve the material as well as spiritual problems of development will speed its overthrow.

The struggle to topple the Stalinist caste in China and the Soviet Union is not the concern only of the Chinese and Soviet peoples. It is of the utmost importance to working people the world over. Similarly, the defeat of American imperialism and its partners and clients is of vital concern to the peoples of China and Russia as well as to American revolutionists. These are not the internal affairs of foreign countries, or somebody else's business. It is one indivisible international fight. In that dual struggle against the oppression of class society and against the Stalinist incubus, a victory anywhere is a victory for working people everywhere.

There are those who will argue that to say such things is to attack China. If this book has accomplished nothing else, I hope that the facts cited have shown that China is today a divided land.

The bureaucracy's survival depends on its capacity to isolate the Chinese masses from the rest of the world. The needs of China's development, the conditions for its future prosperity, and for the establishment of democracy and of socialism lie in the opposite direction.

The Chinese people have demonstrated their capacity to deal with imperialism. They are learning how to face up to the domestic obstacle to their aspirations. And there is no reason to suppose that they will not in time likewise succeed in this emancipatory endeavor.

Notes

Introduction

1. From *Imperial China*, edited by Franz Schurmann and Orville Schell (New York: Vintage Books, 1967), pp. 105, 107-8.

Chapter 2. The Death of Chou En-lai and the Tien An Men Demonstrations

1. Reprinted in *China Quarterly* (number 66, June 1976), pp. 411-16.
2. From the Chinese government's account of the Tien An Men events, "Counter-Revolutionary Political Incident at Tien An Men Square," in *China Quarterly* (number 67, September 1976), p. 665.
3. From ibid., p. 663.
4. From ibid., p. 670.

Chapter 3. The "Gang of Four"

1. *Monthly Review,* October 1976.
2. *New York Times,* September 10, 1976.
3. Hsinhua, October 31, 1966.
4. *New York Times,* October 16, 1976.
5. Hsinhua, November 23-24, 1976.
6. Ibid., December 17, 1976.
7. Ibid., October 24-25, 1976.
8. *New York Times,* October 16, 1976.
9. Hsinhua, October 24-25, 1976.
10. Ibid., October 24-25, 1976.
11. Ibid., October 24-25, 1976.
12. Ibid., October 26, 1976.
13. Ibid., October 26, 1976.
14. Ibid., November 10, 1976.
15. Ibid., November 13, 1976.
16. Ibid., November 13, 1976.
17. Ibid., November 14-15, 1976.
18. Ibid., October 25, 1977.

Chapter 5. Achievements of the Chinese Revolution

1. Harold Isaacs, *The Tragedy of the Chinese Revolution* (New York: Atheneum, 1968), p. 27.
2. Joshua S. Horn, *Away With All Pests* (New York: Monthly Review Press, 1969), p. 125.
3. John G. Gurley, *China's Economy and the Maoist Strategy* (New York: Monthly Review Press, 1976), pp. 13-14.
4. Ruth Gamberg, *Red and Expert: Education in the People's Republic of China* (New York: Schocken Books, 1977), p. 38n.
5. Robert M. Worth, "Health and Medicine" in Yuan-li Wu, ed., *China: A Handbook* (New York: Praeger Publishers, 1973), p. 658.
6. Ibid., p. 662.
7. Horn, *Away With All Pests*, p. 144.
8. Barry Richman, *Industrial Society in Communist China* (New York: Vintage Books, 1969), p. 608.
9. Horn, *Away With All Pests*, p. 49.

Chapter 6. China's Industrial Growth

1. Gurley, *China's Economy and the Maoist Strategy*, p. 15.
2. Chou En-lai, "Report on the Work of the Government," *Peking Review*, January 24, 1975.
3. Hsinhua, October 25, 1977.
4. Barry Richman, *Industrial Society in Communist China* (New York: Vintage Books, 1969), p. 623.
5. Ibid., p. 623.
6. Arthur G. Ashbrook, Jr., "China: Economic Overview" in Joint Economic Committee, U.S. Congress, *China: A Reassessment of the Economy* (Washington: U.S. Government Printing Office, 1975), p. 43.
7. Figures from *Far Eastern Economic Review*, October 3, 1975; *Asia 1977 Yearbook* (Hong Kong: Far Eastern Economic Review, 1977), p. 159; and *Far Eastern Economic Review*, October 7, 1977.
8. *Far Eastern Economic Review*, January 6, 1978.
9. *China Quarterly* (number 70, June 1977), p. 382; *Asia 1977 Yearbook*, p. 159.

Chapter 7. Agricultural Production and Population

1. Based on data in *The Statesman's Year-Book* (New York: St. Martin's Press, 1973), pp. 540, 564, 1398, 1409, 817.
2. Chou En-lai, "Report on the Work of the Government," *Peking Review*, January 24, 1975.
3. See Peter Schran, *The Development of Chinese Agriculture 1950-1959* (Urbana: University of Illinois Press, 1969), pp. 97-101.
4. Cited in ibid., p. 97.
5. Yuan-li Wu, *An Economic Survey of Communist China* (New York: Bookman Associates, 1956), pp. 164-65.
6. Cited in Schran, p. 98.

7. Cited in ibid., p. 99n.

8. K.S. Karol, *China: The Other Communism* (New York: Hill and Wang, 1968), p. 445.

9. Cited by Ralph W. Huenemann in "Urban Rationing in Communist China," *China Quarterly* (number 26, April-June 1966), p. 48.

10. Toronto *Globe and Mail*, November 21, 1977.

11. Figures approximated from Alva Lewis Erisman, "China: Agriculture in the 1970's," in Joint Economic Committee, U.S. Congress, *China: A Reassessment of the Economy* (Washington: U.S. Government Printing Office, 1975), p. 343.

12. *Far Eastern Economic Review*, May 6, 1977.

13. *The Varsity* (University of Toronto student newspaper), November 2, 1977.

14. The 1957 figure is given in Huenemann, "Urban Rationing in Communist China," *China Quarterly* (number 26, April-June 1966), p. 48.

Chapter 8. The Overall Growth of Social Wealth

1. Arthur G. Ashbrook, Jr., "China: Economic Overview, 1975" in Joint Economic Committee, U.S. Congress, *China: A Reassessment of the Economy* (Washington: U.S. Government Printing Office, 1975), p. 24.

2. Carl Riskin, "Judging Economic Development: The Case of China," *Economic and Political Weekly* (Bombay), October 8, 1977, p. 1742.

3. Ibid., pp. 1742-43.

4. *Asia 1977 Yearbook* (Hong Kong: Far Eastern Economic Review, 1977), p. 76.

5. Subramanian Swamy, "The Economic Distance Between China and India, 1955-73," *China Quarterly* (number 70, June 1977), p. 373.

6. Ibid., p. 373.

7. Gurley, *China's Economy and the Maoist Strategy*, p. 189.

8. Hsinhua, October 25, 1977.

9. *Guardian*, March 2, 1977.

10. Ibid.

11. *Far Eastern Economic Review*, October 7, 1977.

Chapter 9. The Privileged Caste

1. Simon Leys, *Chinese Shadows* (New York: Viking Press, 1977), p. 117.

2. Charles Bettelheim, *Class Struggles in the USSR: First Period, 1917-1923* (New York: Monthly Review Press, 1976), pp. 164-65; and E.H. Carr, *The Bolshevik Revolution 1917-1923*, vol. 2 (Harmondsworth, England: Penguin Books, 1966), pp. 177-79.

3. Cited in Martin King Whyte, "Inequality and Stratification in China," *China Quarterly* (number 64, December 1975), p. 685.

4. Chow Ching-wen, *Ten Years of Storm* (New York: Holt, Rinehart and Winston, 1960), p. 182.

5. Ibid., pp. 185-86.

6. Roxane Witke, *Comrade Chiang Ch'ing* (Boston: Little, Brown and Company, 1977), pp. 37-38.

7. Ibid., p. 38.

8. Ibid., p. 38.

9. Ibid., p. 42.

10. Ibid., p. 42.

11. Ibid., p. 119.

12. Ibid., pp. 501-2n.

13. Ibid., p. 290.

14. Toronto *Globe and Mail*, March 4, 1975.

Chapter 10. Peking's Foreign Policy

1. *The Amerasia Papers: A Clue to the Catastrophe of China* (Washington: U.S. Government Printing Office, 1970), vol. II, p. 1144.

2. Ibid., p. 1145.

3. "Study Prepared by the Department of Defense," *United States–Vietnam Relations, 1945-1967* (Washington: U.S. Government Printing Office, 1971), Book 1, Part III. C., pp. C-1, C-2.

4. Cited in Donald Hindley, *The Communist Party of Indonesia, 1951-1963* (Berkeley: University of California Press, 1964), p. 286.

5. Hsinhua, May 23, 1965.

6. *Le Monde*, April 14, 1971.

7. *Ceylon News*, June 3, 1971.

8. United Press International dispatch, August 5, 1971.

9. *Guardian*, May 5, 1976.

10. Leon Trotsky, "The Bonapartist Philosophy of the State" (May 1, 1939), *Writings of Leon Trotsky 1938-39* (New York: Pathfinder Press, 1974), p. 325.

11. *Far Eastern Economic Review*, March 25, 1974.

12. Hsinhua, October 15, 1976.

13. Ibid., October 15, 1976.

14. Cited by George M. Patterson, "Treatment of Minorities," in Werner Klatt (ed.), *The Chinese Model* (Hong Kong, 1965), pp. 154-55.

15. Hsinhua, March 7, 1978.

Chapter 11. The "Two-Line Struggle"

1. *Monthly Review*, June 1974, p. 8.

2. Ibid., p. 9.

3. Paul M. Sweezy and Charles Bettelheim, *On the Transition to Socialism* (New York: Monthly Review Press, 1971), p. 31.

4. *First Five-Year Plan for Development of the People's Republic of China in 1953-1957* (Peking: Foreign Languages Press, 1956), p. 119.

5. Peter Schran, *The Development of Chinese Agriculture, 1950-1959* (Urbana: University of Illinois Press, 1969), p. 29.

6. Ibid., p. 6.

7. Cited by Philip Bridgham, "Factionalism in the Central Committee"

in *Party Leadership and Revolutionary Power in China* (London: Cambridge University Press, 1970), p. 214.

8. Mao Tsetung, "Remarks at the Spring Festival" (February 13, 1964) in Stuart Schram (ed.), *Chairman Mao Talks to the People, Talks and Letters: 1956-1971* (New York: Pantheon, 1974), pp. 210-11.

9. Ibid., p. 288.

10. Jean Daubier, "The Chinese Cultural Revolution," *Monthly Review,* October 1970, p. 35.

11. Karl Marx and Frederick Engels, *Collected Works* (New York: International Publishers, 1975), vol. 3, pp. 294-95. Emphasis in original.

12. Karl Marx, *Grundrisse: Foundations of the Critique of Political Economy (Rough Draft)* (Harmondsworth, England: Penguin Books, 1973), pp. 711-12.

13. V.I. Lenin, "On the Significance of Militant Materialism" (March 12, 1922), *Collected Works* (Moscow: Progress Publishers, 1973), vol. 33, p. 230.

14. Ibid., pp. 232-33.

Chapter 12. Science and Culture— Under Mao and Under Hua

1. *New York Times,* January 3, 1978.
2. Reuters dispatch, January 1, 1978.
3. Hsinhua, January 8-9, 1978.
4. Hsinhua, November 6, 1976.
5. *Washington Post,* May 5, 1977.
6. *Guardian,* March 2, 1977.
7. *New York Times Magazine,* December 4, 1977.
8. *Bulletin of the Atomic Scientists,* September 1977.
9. Toronto *Globe and Mail,* August 29, 1977.
10. *New York Times,* September 2, 1977.
11. Hsinhua, July 17-18, 1977.
12. Hsinhua, March 22, 1977.
13. Hsinhua, November 6, 1976.
14. Hsinhua, November 9, 1976.
15. *China Reconstructs,* July 1977.
16. *Far Eastern Economic Review,* May 20, 1977.
17. Agence France-Presse dispatch, February 23, 1978.
18. Hsinhua, March 15, 1978.

Chapter 13. Justice, Repression, and Political Prisoners

1. Gurley, *China's Economy and the Maoist Strategy,* p. 153.
2. Simon Leys, *Chinese Shadows* (New York: Viking Press, 1977), pp. 3-4.
3. Cited in Roderick MacFarquhar (ed.), *The Hundred Flowers Campaign and the Chinese Intellectuals* (New York: Frederick A. Praeger, 1960), p. 94.

4. Ross Terrill, *800,000,000: The Real China* (Boston: Little, Brown, 1972), p. 100.

5. Toronto *Globe and Mail,* October 8, 1977.

6. Ibid., October 10, 1977.

7. Text in *The Hundred Flowers Campaign and the Chinese Intellectuals,* p. 245.

8. Claudie and Jacques Broyelle and Evelyne Tschirhart, *Deuxième Retour de Chine* (Paris: Editions du Seuil, 1977), p. 78.

9. Ibid., p. 144.

10. Simon Leys, "Broken Images: Conversations in Hong Kong," *Dissent,* Fall 1976.

11. *Deuxième Retour de Chine,* p. 148.

12. Ibid., pp. 148-49.

13. Ibid., p. 149.

14. Cited in ibid., p. 152.

15. V.I. Lenin, "'Dual' Subordination and Legality," *Collected Works,* vol. 33 (Moscow: Foreign Languages Publishing House, 1962), pp. 364-65.

16. Toronto *Globe and Mail,* October 12, 1977.

17. *Deuxième Retour de Chine,* p. 153.

18. Cited in ibid., p. 154.

19. Bao Ruo-wang and Rudolph Chelminski, *Prisoner of Mao* (New York: Coward, McCann & Geoghegan, 1973), pp. 86-87.

20. Ibid., pp. 99-100.

21. Li Fu-jen and Peng Shu-tse, *Revolutionaries in Mao's Prisons* (New York: Pathfinder Press, 1974), pp. 8, 9, 12.

22. London *Guardian,* November 9, 1977.

23. *Prisoner of Mao,* pp. 10-11n.

24. Ibid., p. 11n.

25. *New York Times,* March 29, 1977.

26. Cited in *Christian Science Monitor,* January 6, 1978.

27. Cited in *New York Times,* February 25, 1978.

28. Hsinhua, March 15, 1978.

29. Ibid., May 27, 1978.

30. Ibid., June 11-12, 1978.

31. Toronto *Globe and Mail,* May 22, 1978; *New York Times,* June 6, 1978.

Chapter 14. Signs of Instability

1. *Washington Post,* November 24, 1976.

2. Ibid., December 10, 1976.

3. *New York Times,* January 1, 1977.

4. Ibid., December 15, 1976.

5. *Chicago Tribune,* December 30, 1976.

6. *Far Eastern Economic Review,* October 7, 1977.

7. *Le Monde,* April 14, 1977.

8. Reuters dispatch, November 14, 1976.

9. *Le Monde,* May 24-25, 1977.

10. Ibid., August 13, 1977.
11. Toronto *Globe and Mail,* November 1, 1977.

Chapter 15. The New Party Leadership

1. Hsinhua, August 21-22, 1977.
2. Ibid., August 23, 1977.
3. Ibid., August 21-22, 1977.
4. Ibid., March 6, 1978.

Chapter 16. The Case of Li I-che

1. *New York Times,* August 30, 1977.
2. *The Revolution Is Dead, Long Live the Revolution* (Hong Kong: The Seventies Biweekly, 1976), p. 250.
3. Ibid., p. 253.
4. Ibid., pp. 256-57.
5. Ibid., p. 257.
6. Ibid., pp. 263, 264.
7. Ibid., p. 270.
8. Ibid., p. 278.
9. Ibid., p. 279.
10. Ibid., pp. 279, 280.
11. Ibid., p. 280.
12. Ibid., p. 281.
13. *Le Monde,* May 11, 1977.
14. *Far Eastern Economic Review,* July 15, 1977.
15. *Rouge,* April 30, 1977.

Index

Agriculture: and arable land, 65-66; crisis, 114-16; forced collectivization, 115; Mao on, 73-74; policy during Great Leap Forward, 66-67, 73, 74; prerevolutionary, 63n; production, 66-70, 72; productivity, 64, 66

Aidit, D. N., 97, 98

Alonso, Alicia, 132

Art and literature; Chiang Ch'ing on, 19, 22, 26; policy during Cultural Revolution, 126, 127-28, 129-31; policy under Hua, 127, 133-36

Backhouse, Sir Edmund, 9

Bandaranaike, Sirimavo, 100, 101

Bao Ruo-wang (Jean Pasqualini), 146, 147, 148, 151

Benton, Greg, 150

Bettelheim, Charles, 110

Bolshevik Party, 13, 86, 178

Brandt, Willi, 102

Brazil, 77

Brezhnev, Leonid, 102

Brown, David, 72

Broyelle, Claudie and Jacques, 141-43

Buck, John Lossing, 70

Bureaucratic methods: in CCP, 32-37, 152-53; used by Mao, 32, 34; in Soviet Union, 85

Bureaucratic privilege, 29-30, 85-90, 173-74

Burns, John, 89

Butterfield, Fox, 130, 168

Capital (Marx), 122

Capital punishment, 160-61

Center of the World: Communism and the Mind of China (Elegant), 138n

Chang Ch'un-ch'iao, 26, 29, 35. *See also* "Gang of four"

Ch'en Hsi-lien, 165

Ch'en I-yang, 169, 175

Ch'en Po-ta, 28

Ch'en Tu-hsiu, 150

Cheng Chao-lin, 150-51

Chiang Ch'ing: career, 27-28; charges against, 17-18, 29-30, 31, 34, 35; lifestyle, 87-89; and Mao, 38n; memoirs, 87-89; policy on art, 19, 22, 26. *See also* "Gang of four"

Chiang Kai-shek, 11, 20, 104; and CCP, 92, 93-94, 162

Chile, 102

Ch'in Shih Hwang, 7, 23-24n, 119, 120

China Democratic League, 86

China Reconstructs (Peking), 134

China's Economy and the Maoist Strategy (Gurley), 49

Chinese Communist Party (CCP): agriculture policy, 114-15; attitude to U.S. imperialism, 93-94; compared to Bolshevik Party, 86, 178; Central Committee, 163, 164, 166; congresses, 162-66; factions, 26-27, 41, 110, 113-14, 117-19; history, 92-94, 114; persecution of Trotskyists, 149-51; Politburo, 26, 163, 165, 166; Politburo Standing Committee, 163-164; relations with Chiang Kai-shek, 93-94, 162

Chinese Human Rights Society, 175, 176

187